Color and Trace

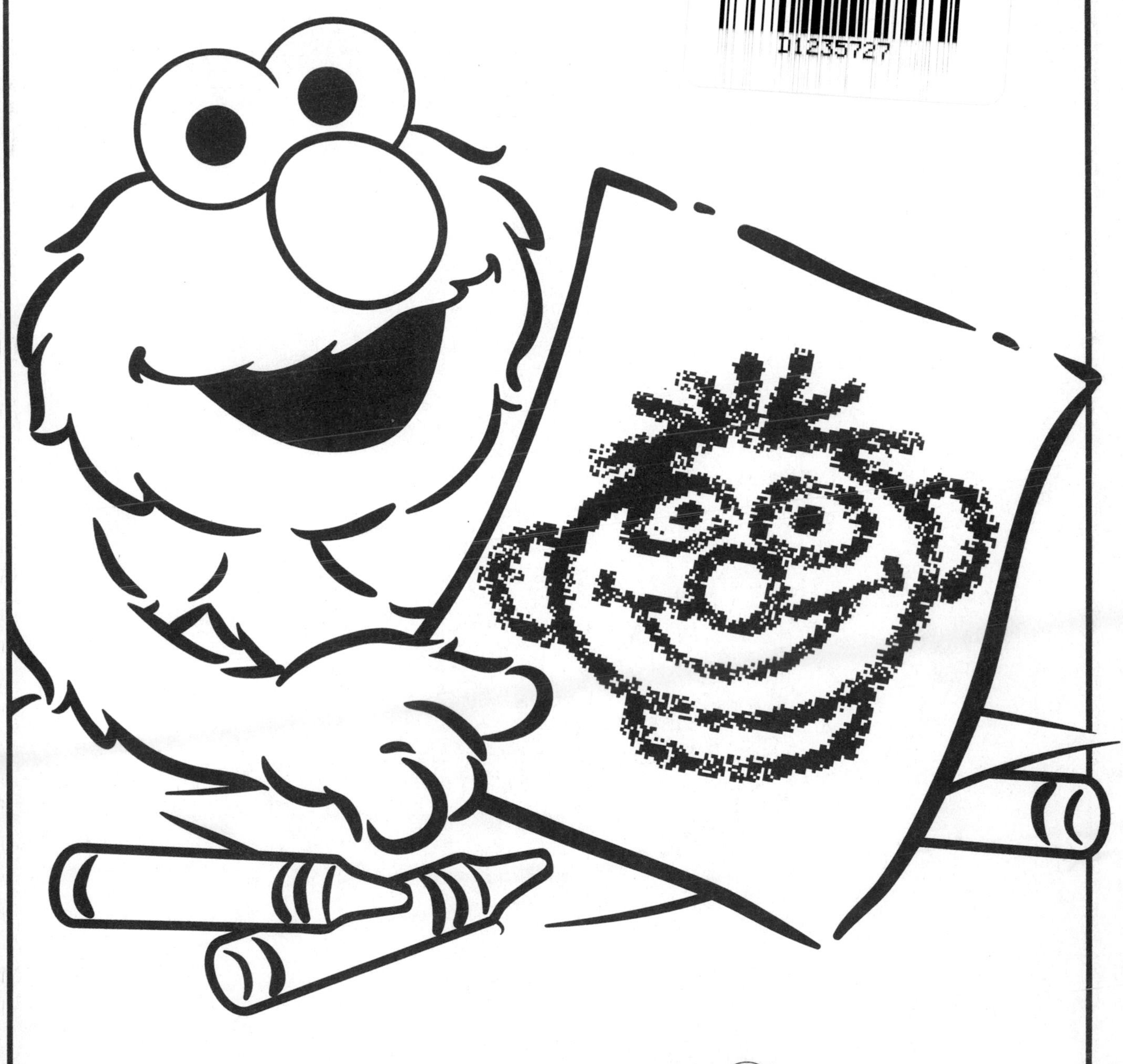

SESAME STREET

bendon

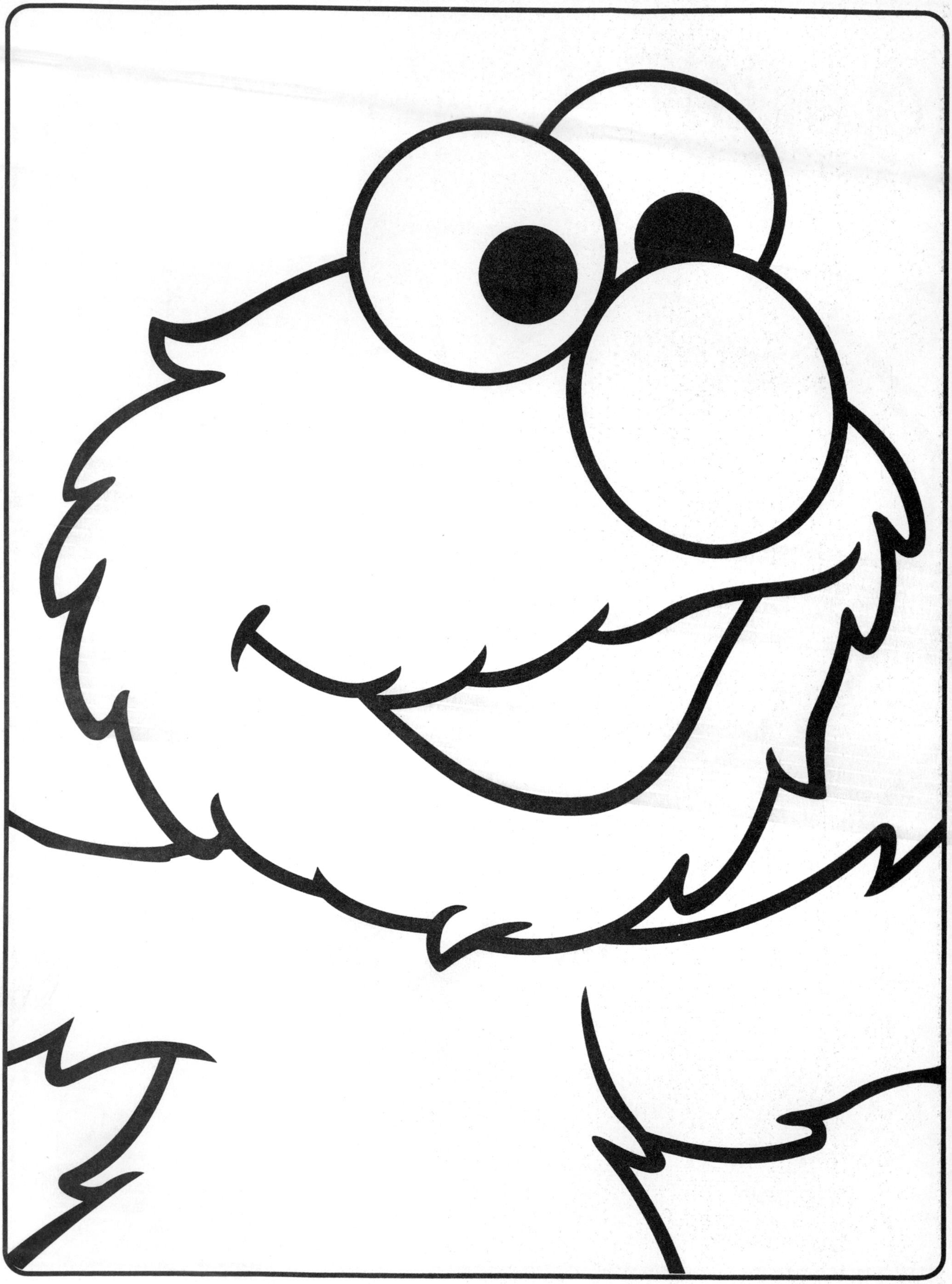

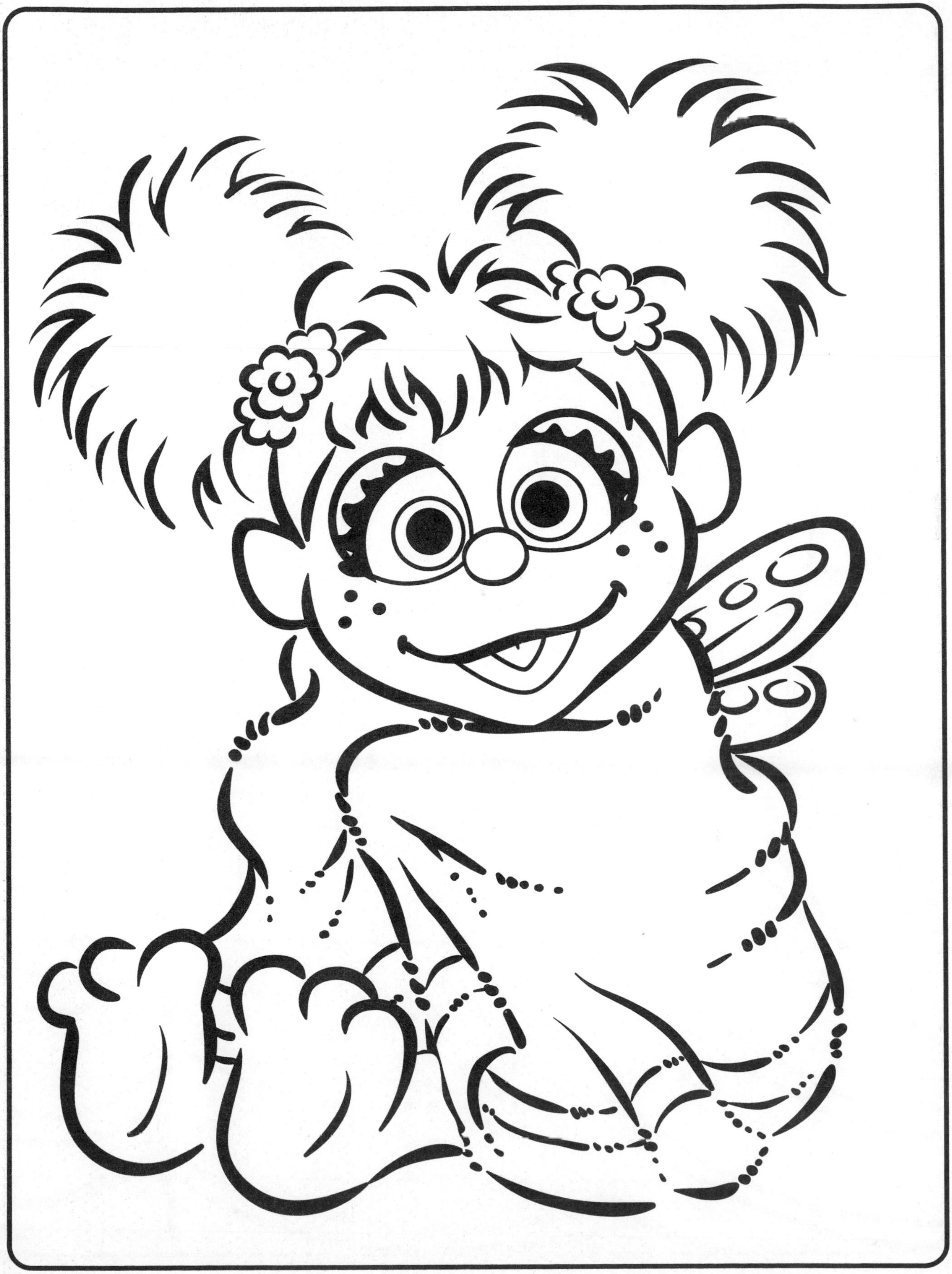

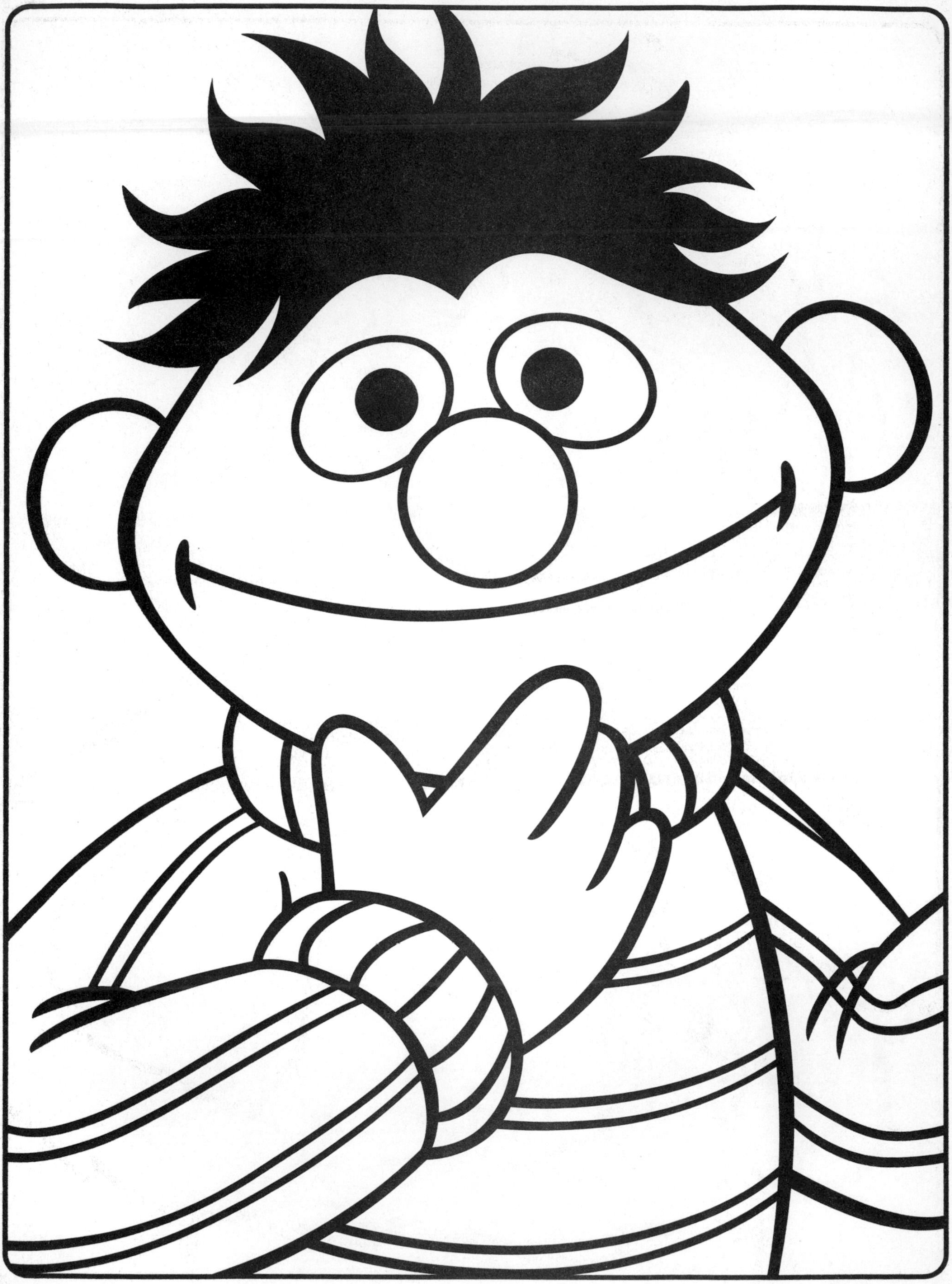

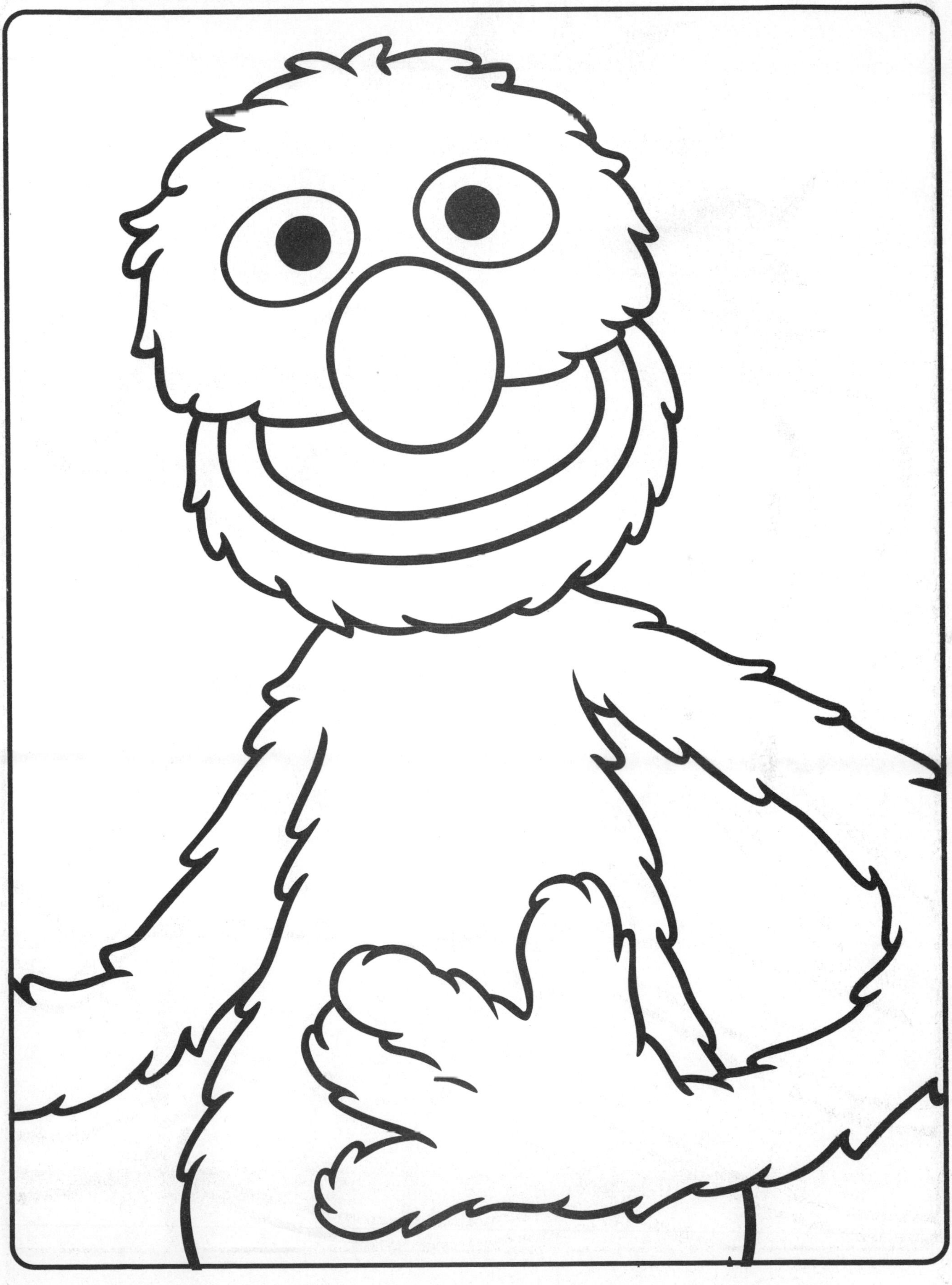

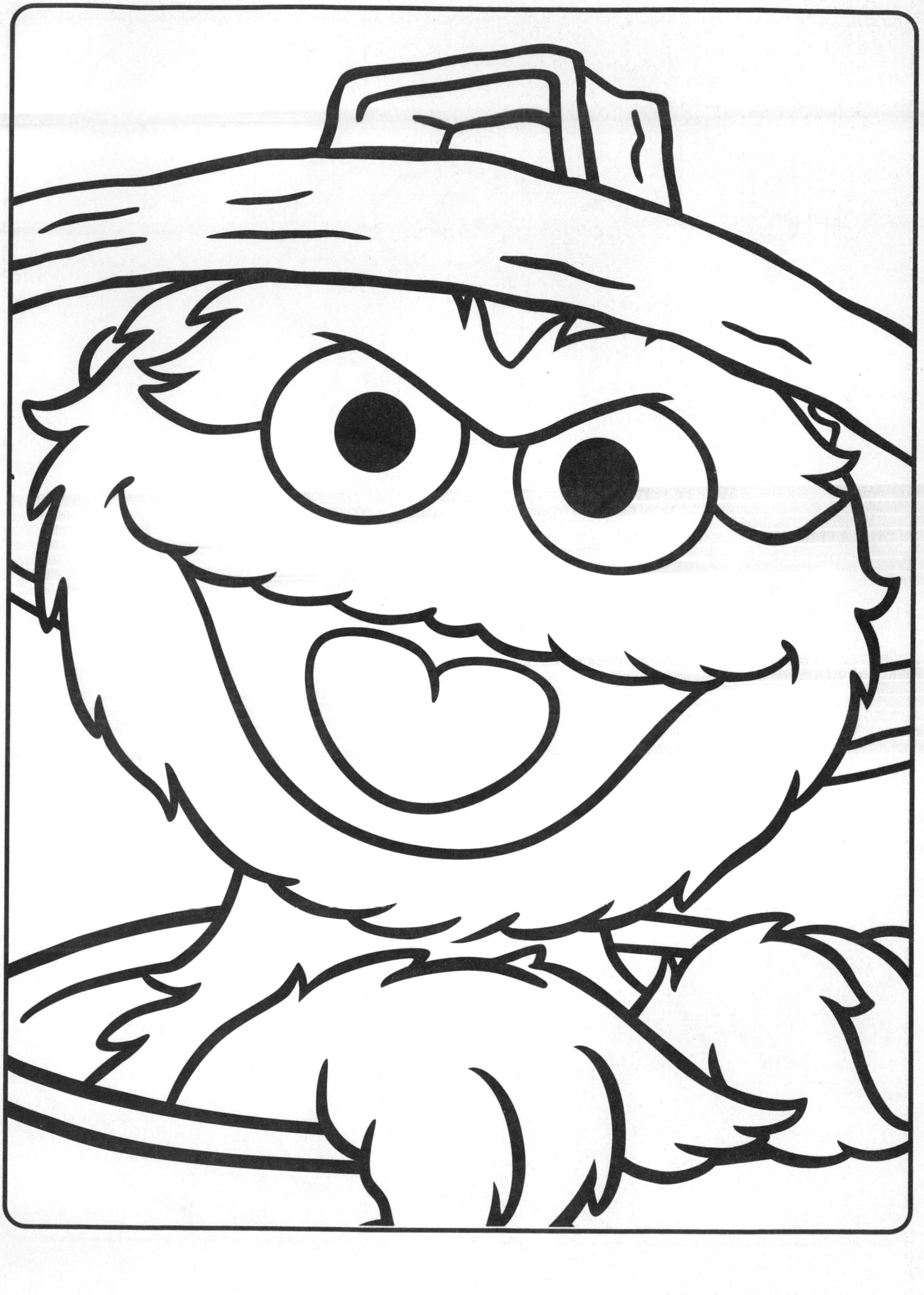

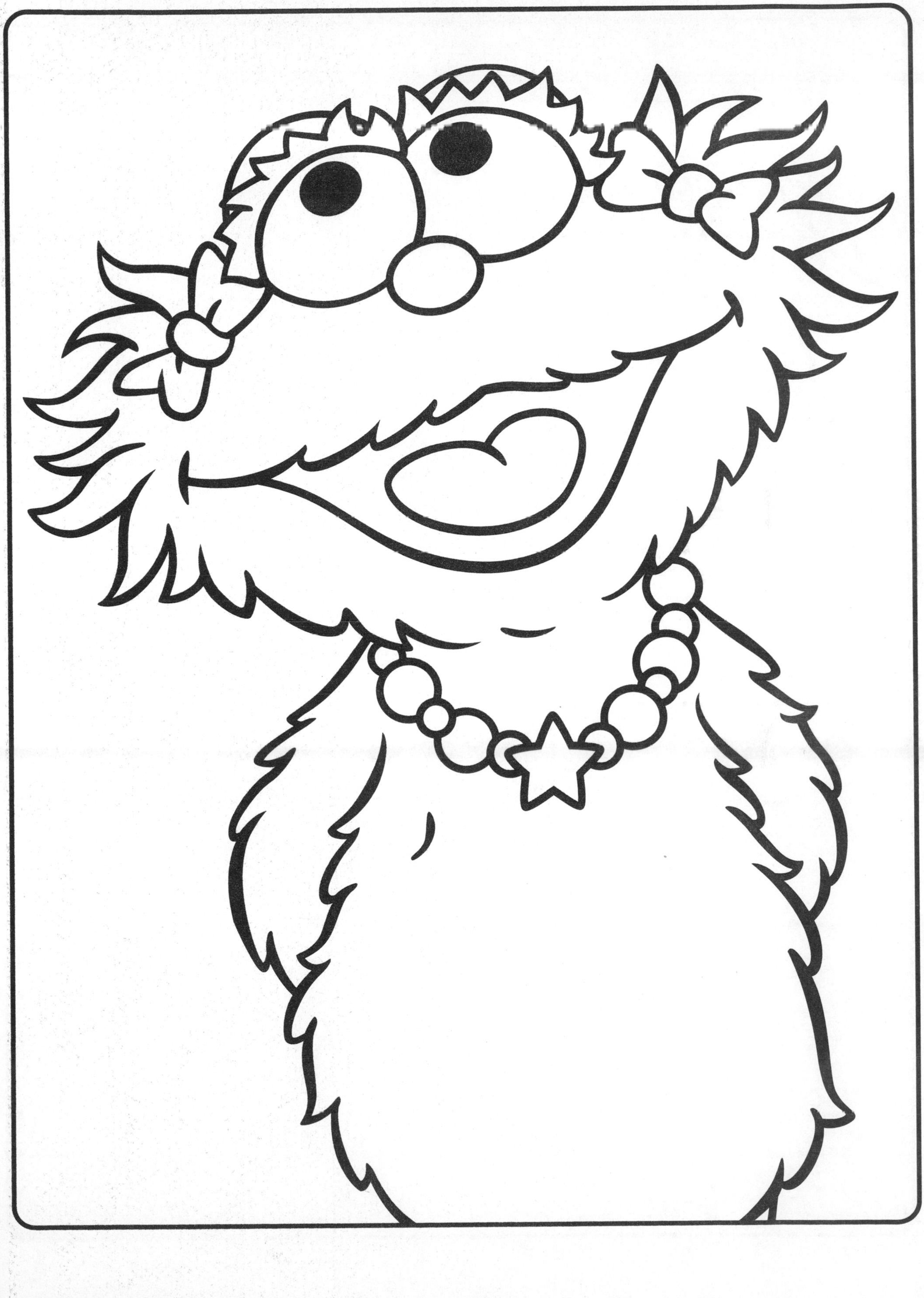

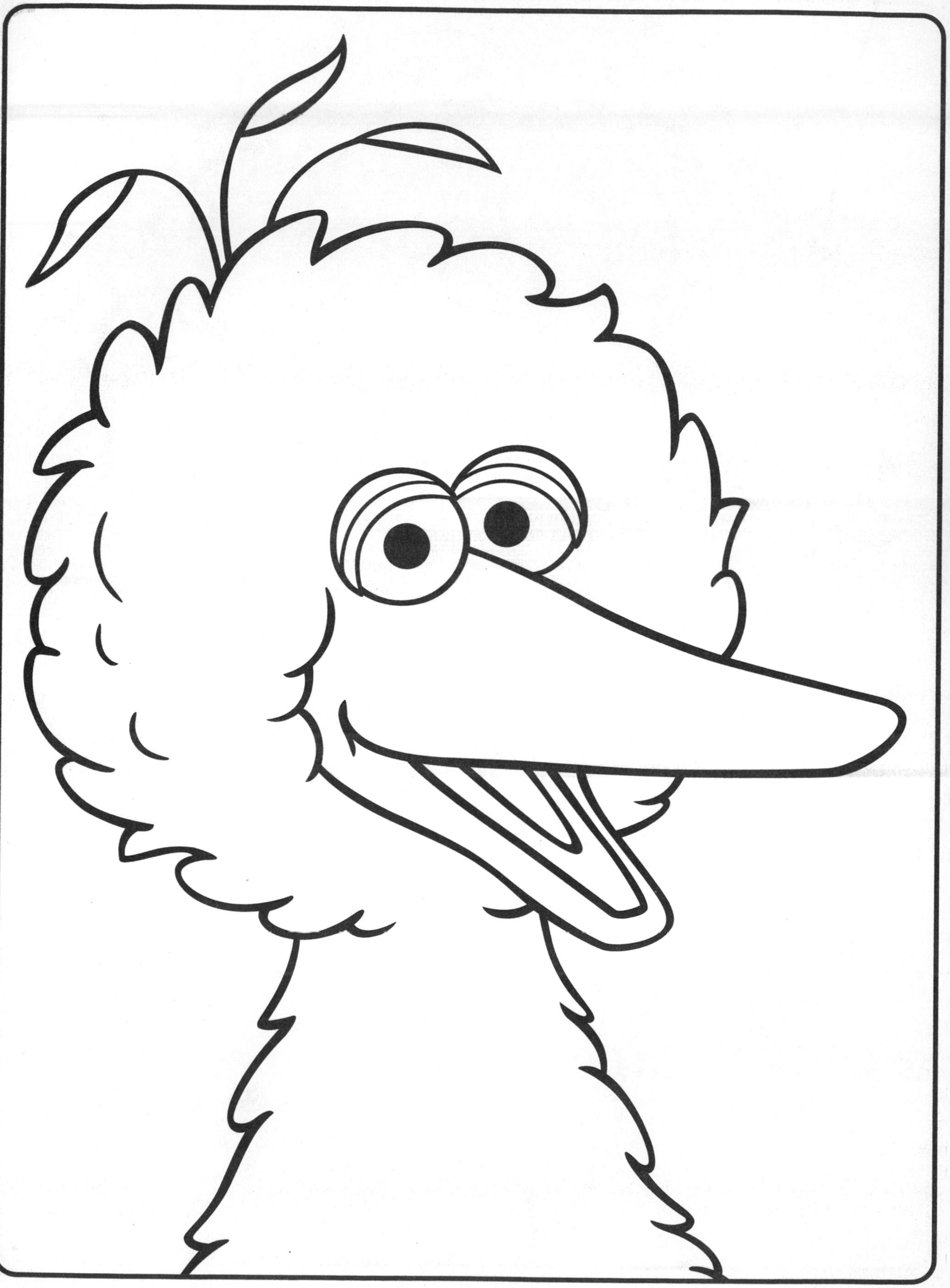

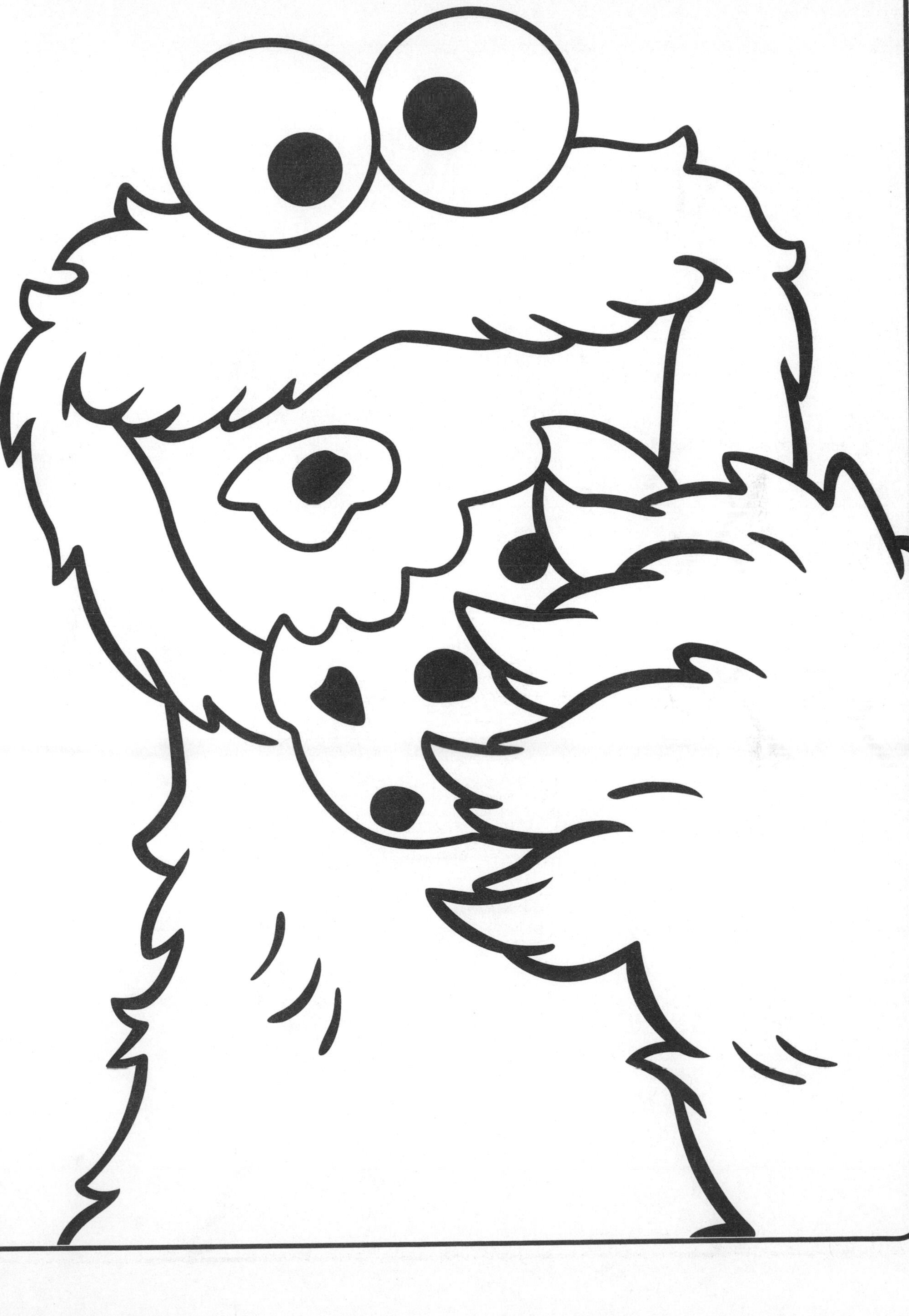

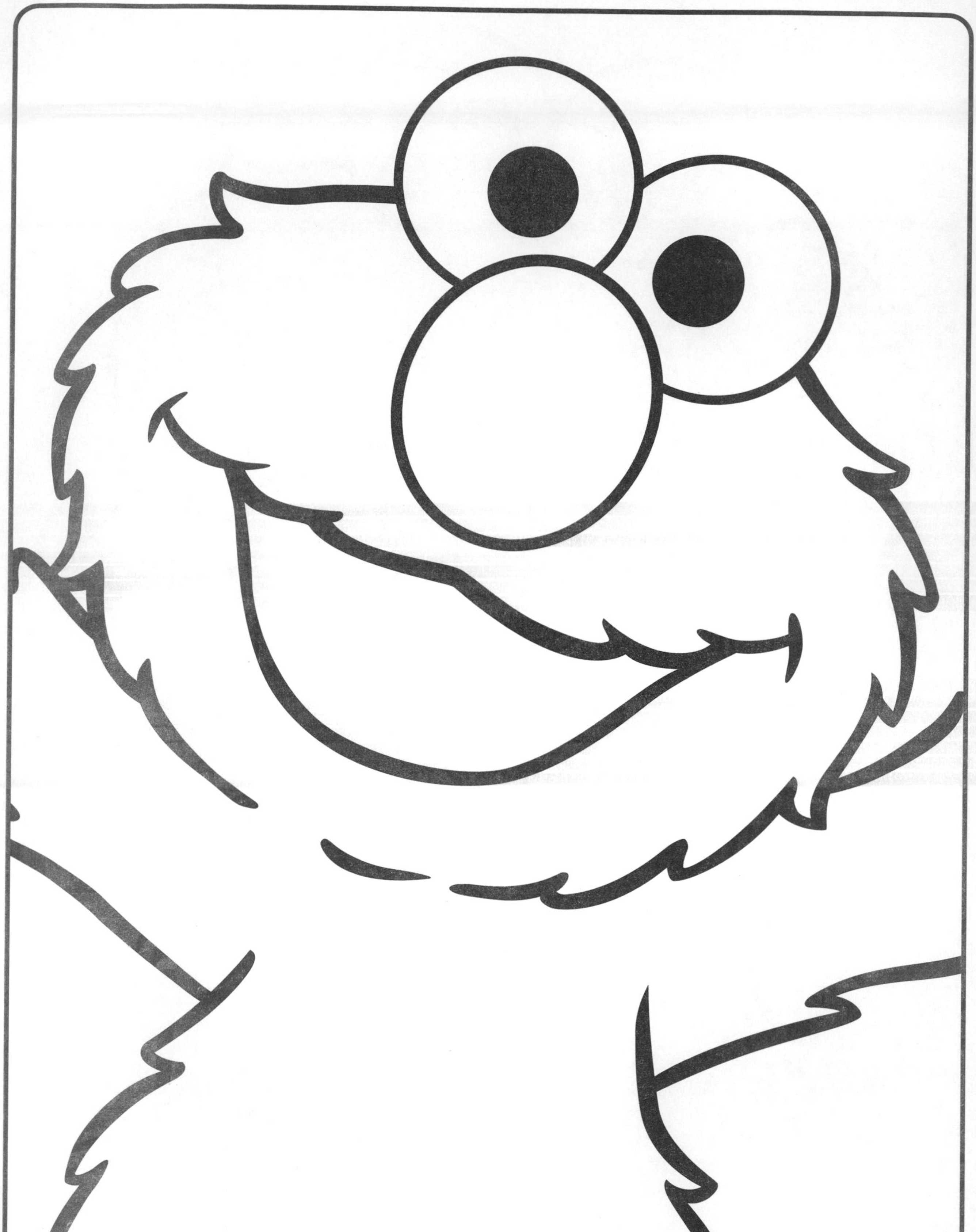

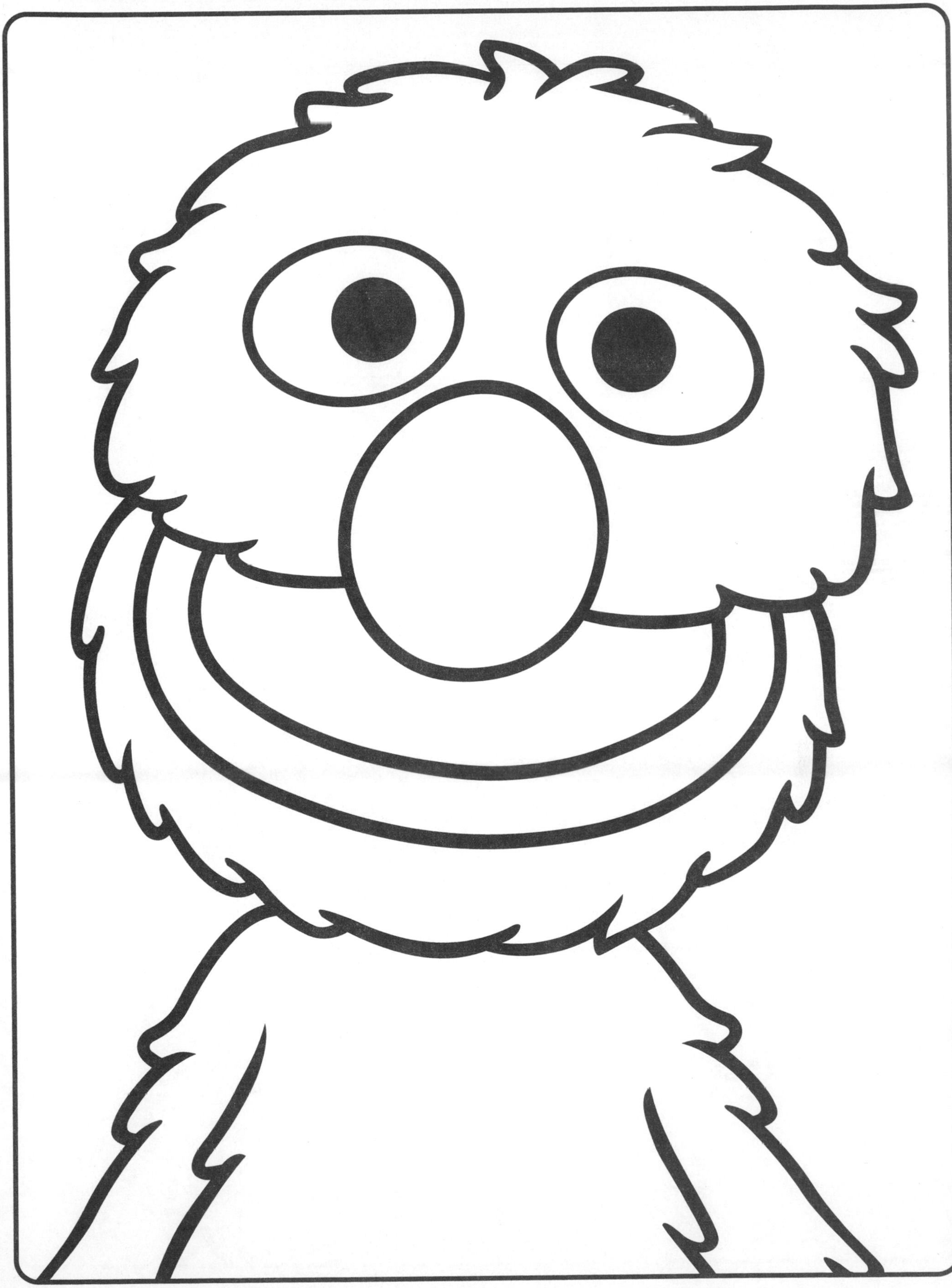

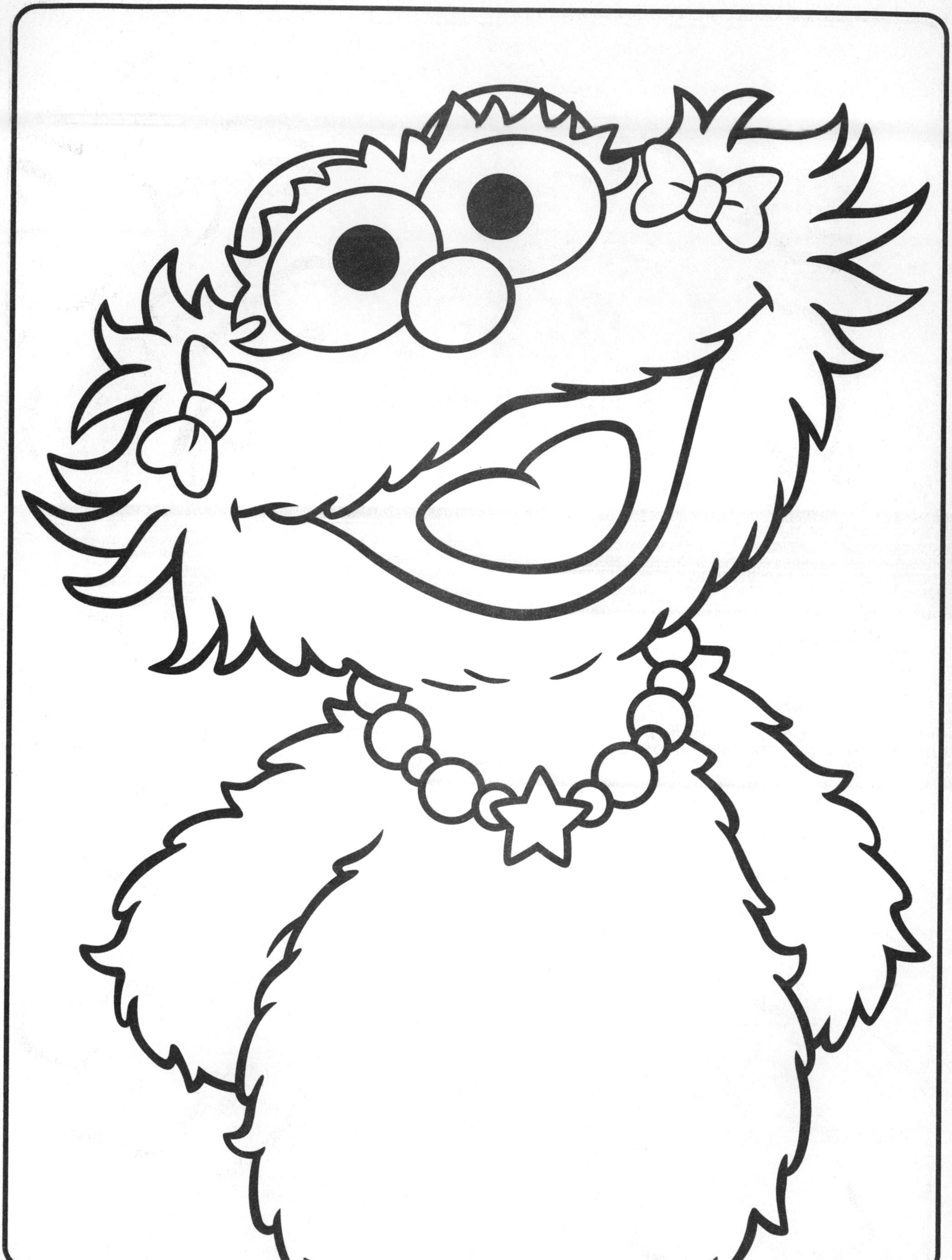

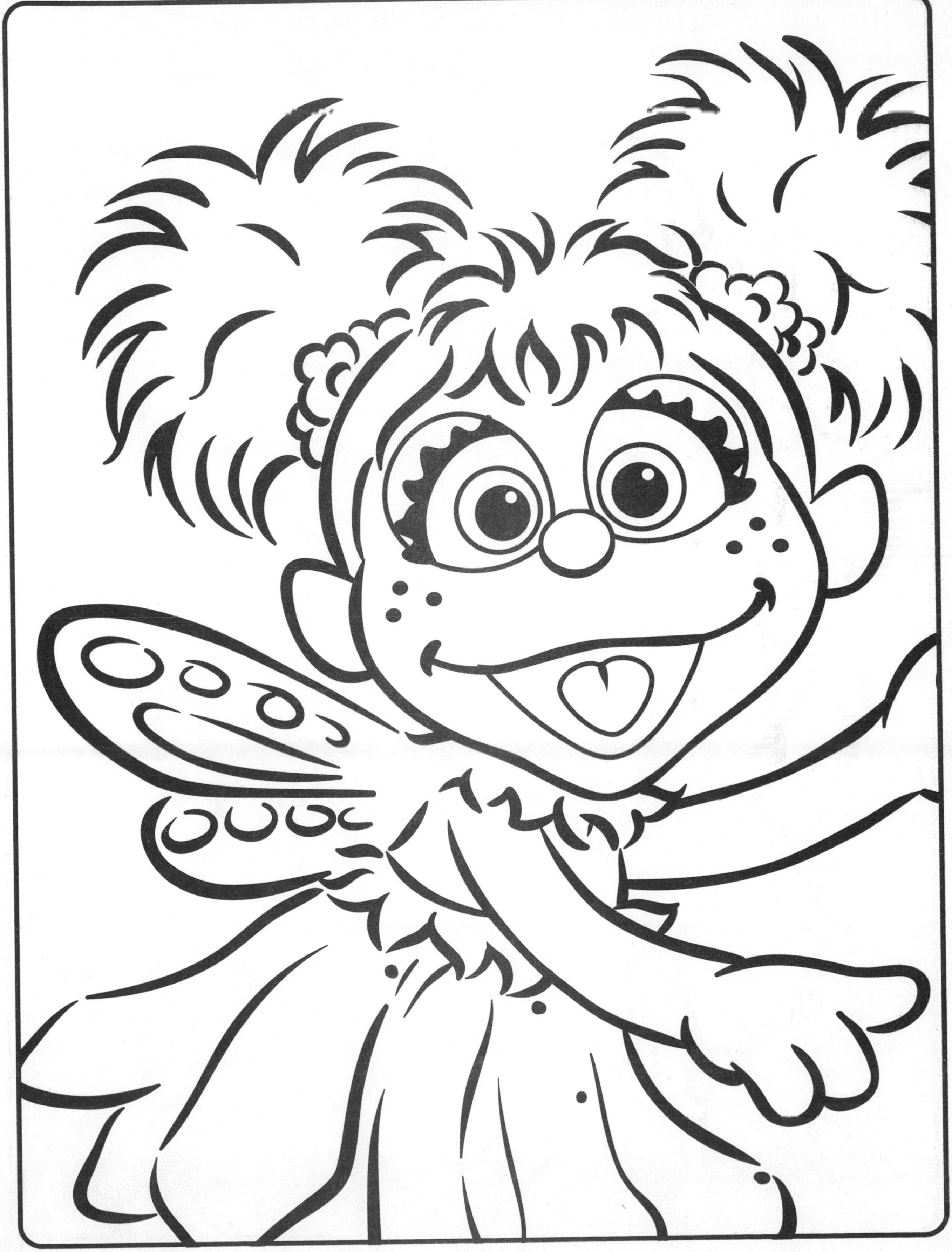

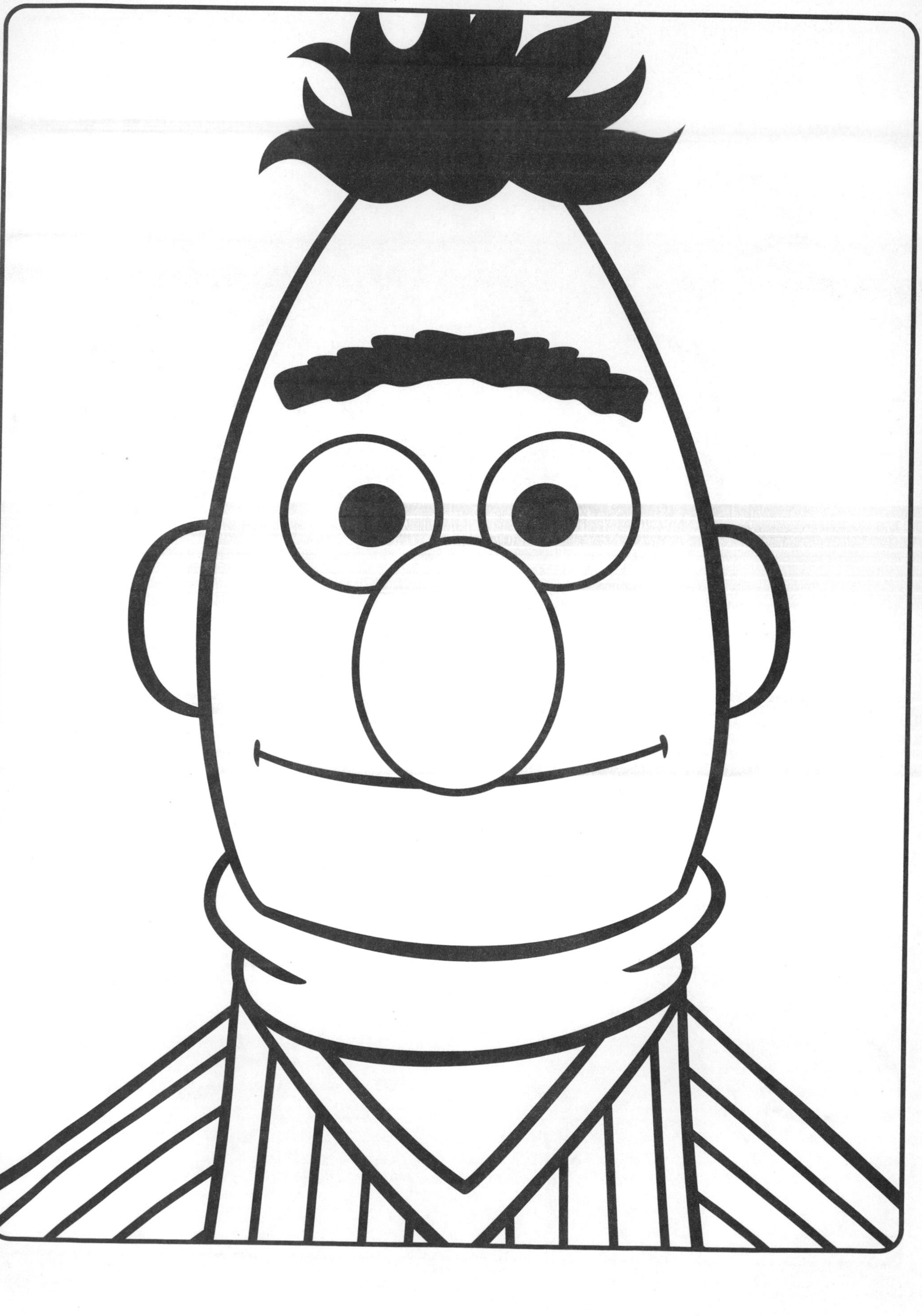

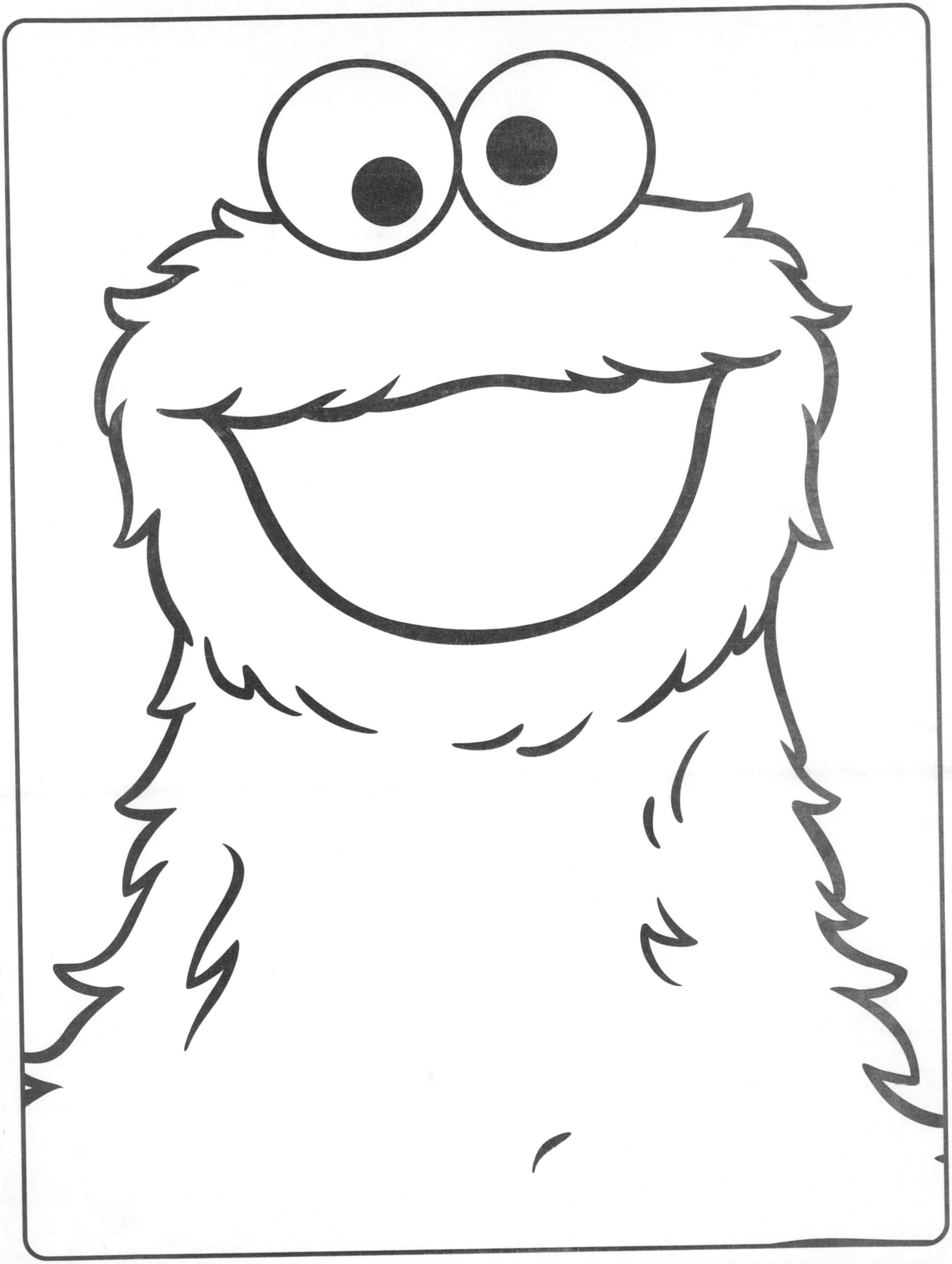

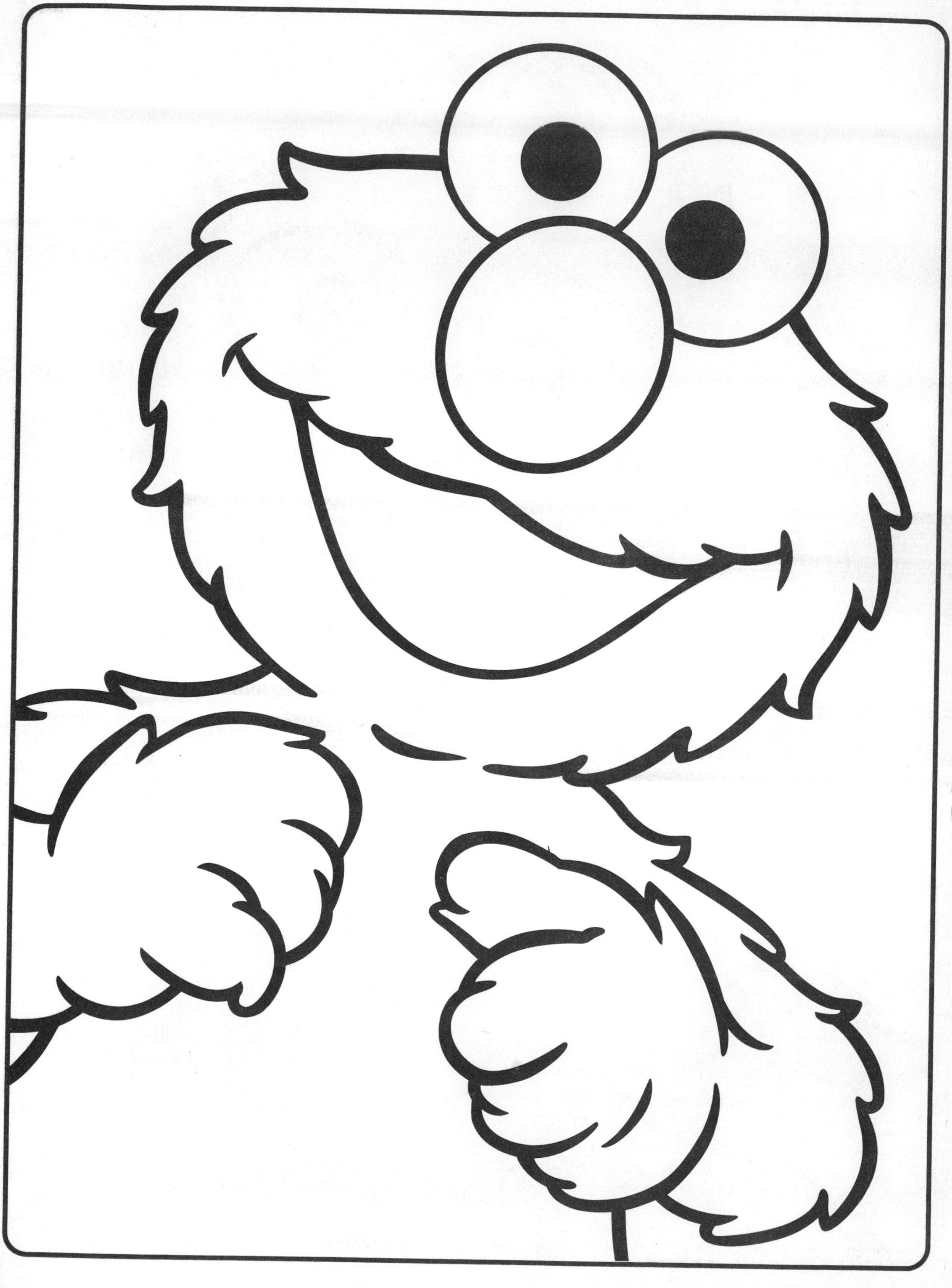

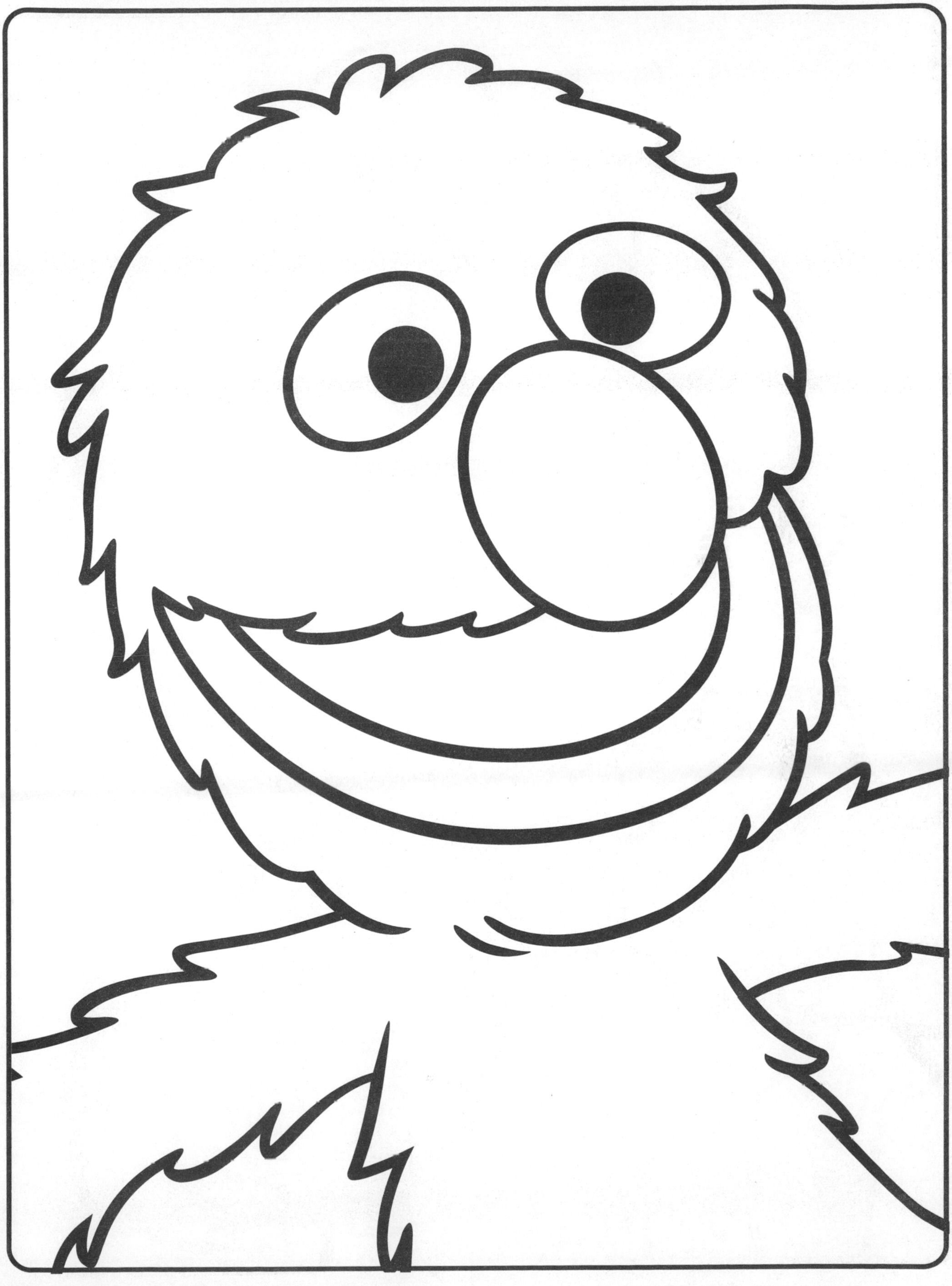

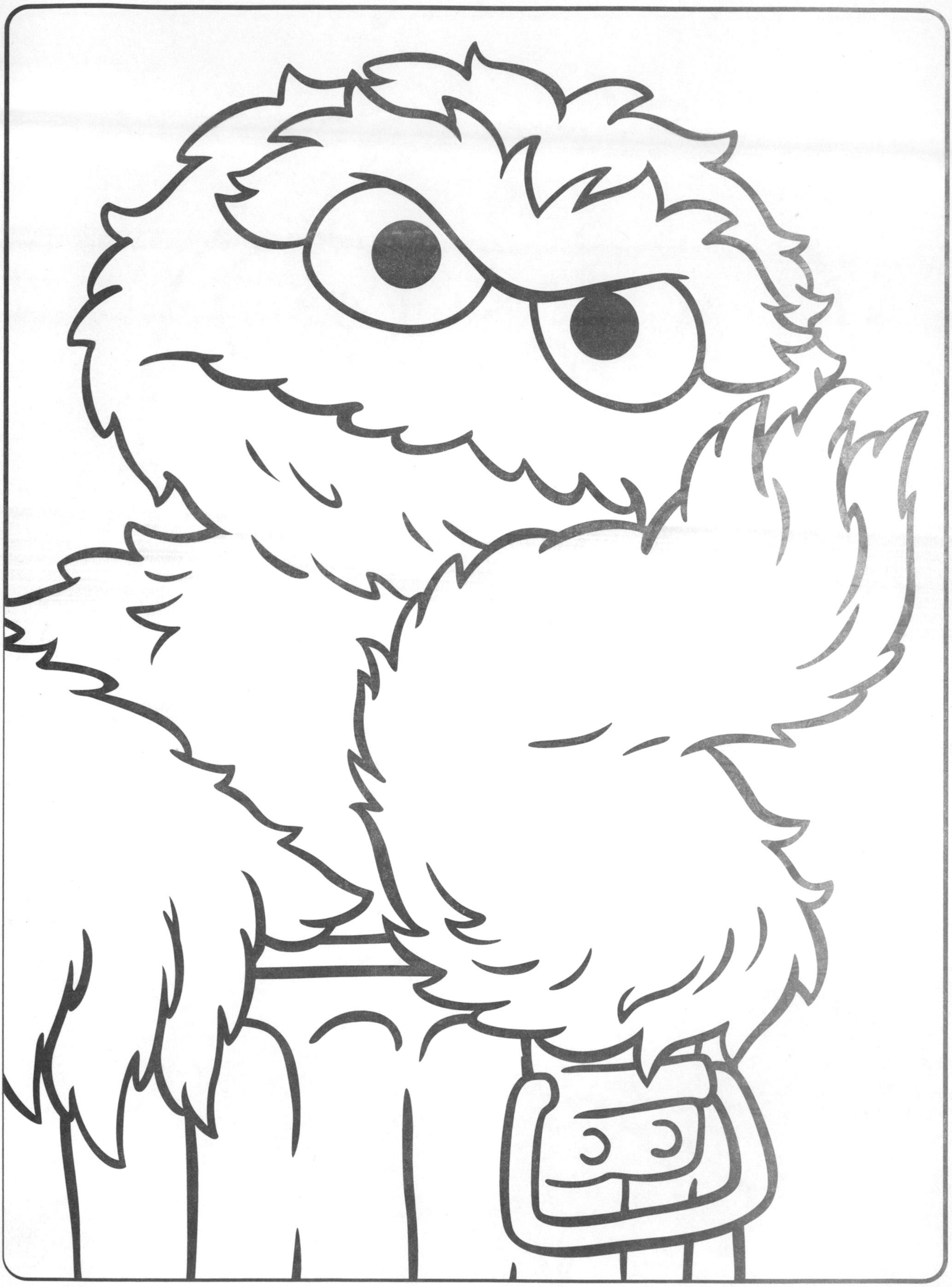

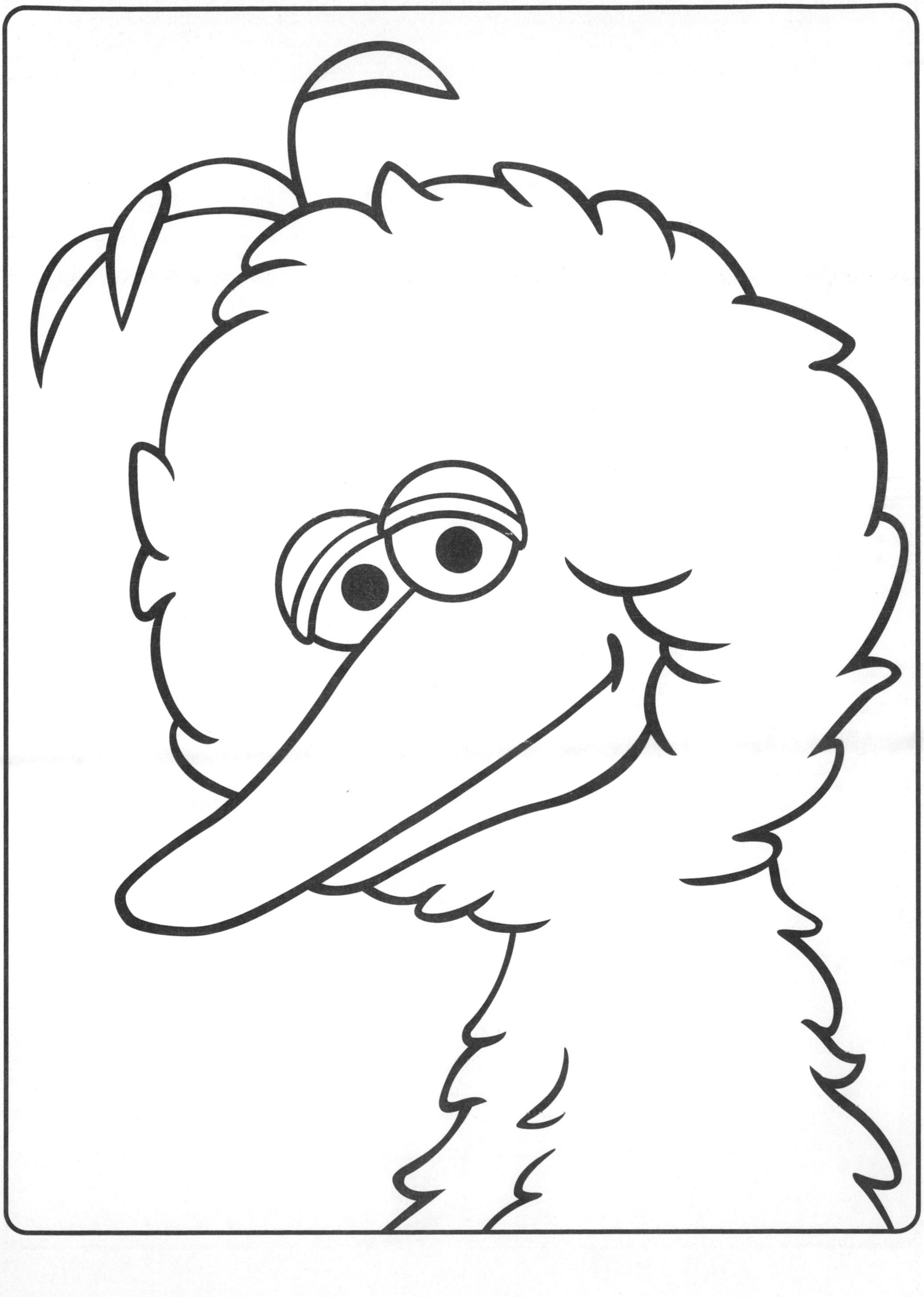

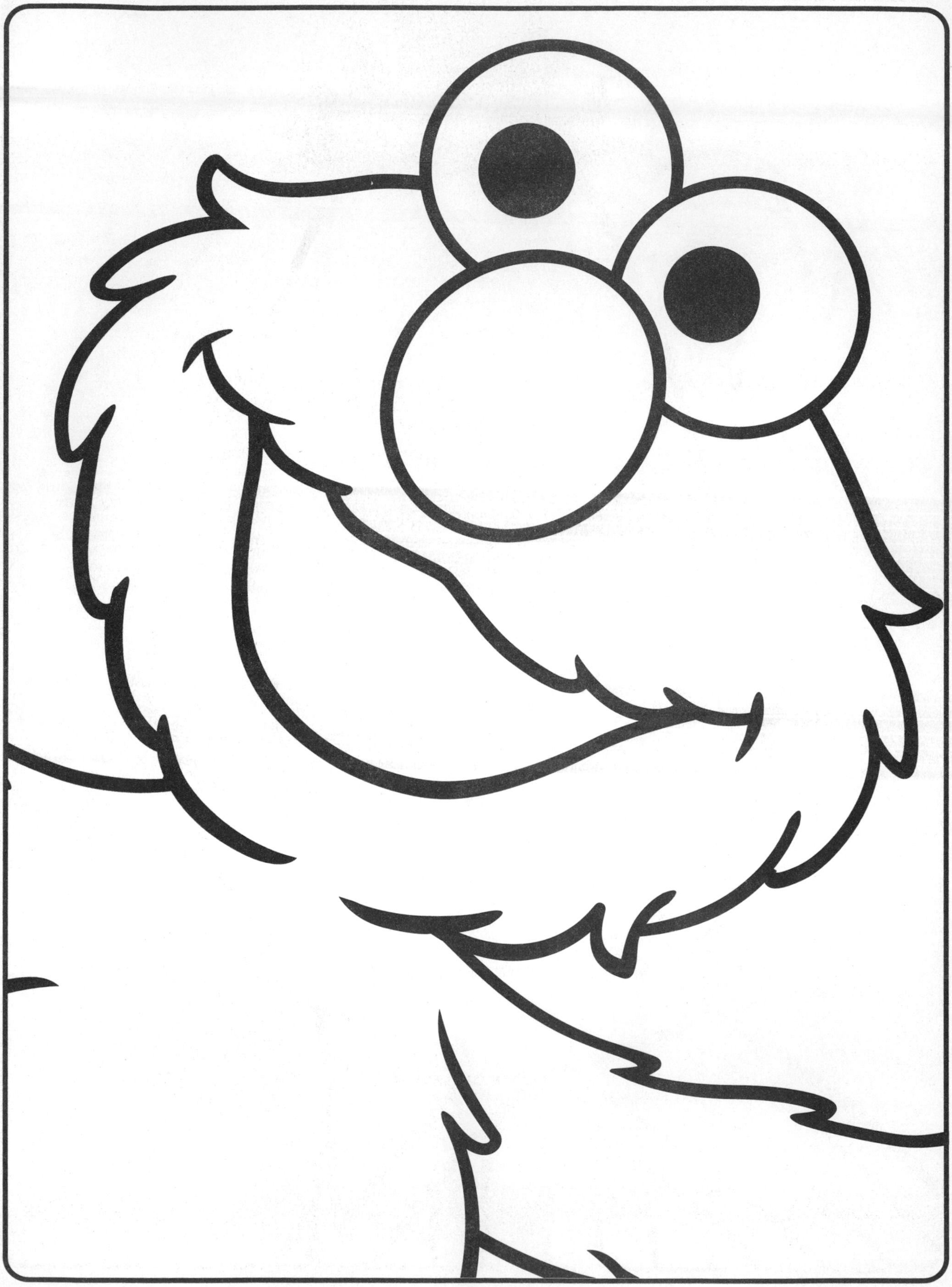

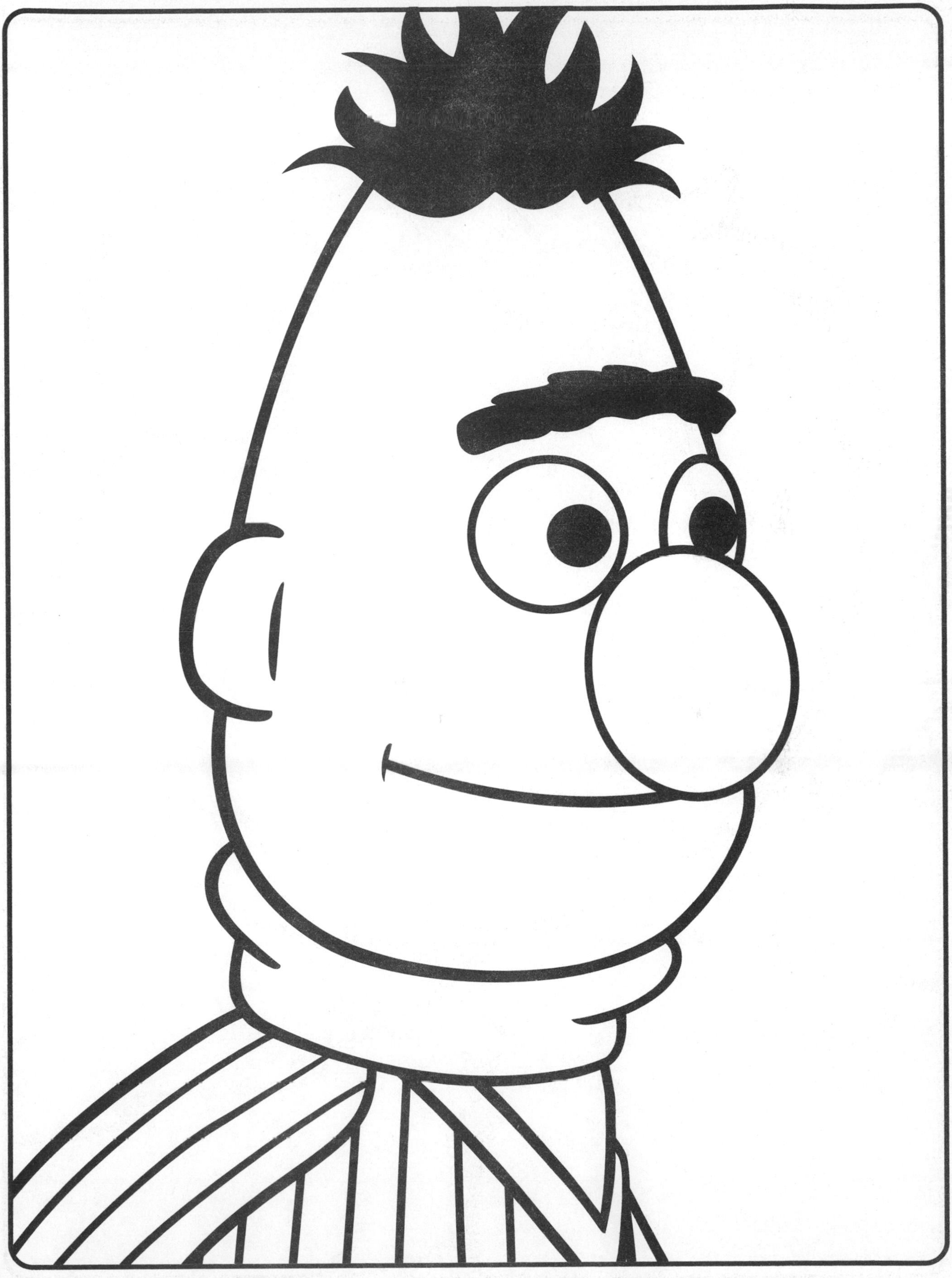

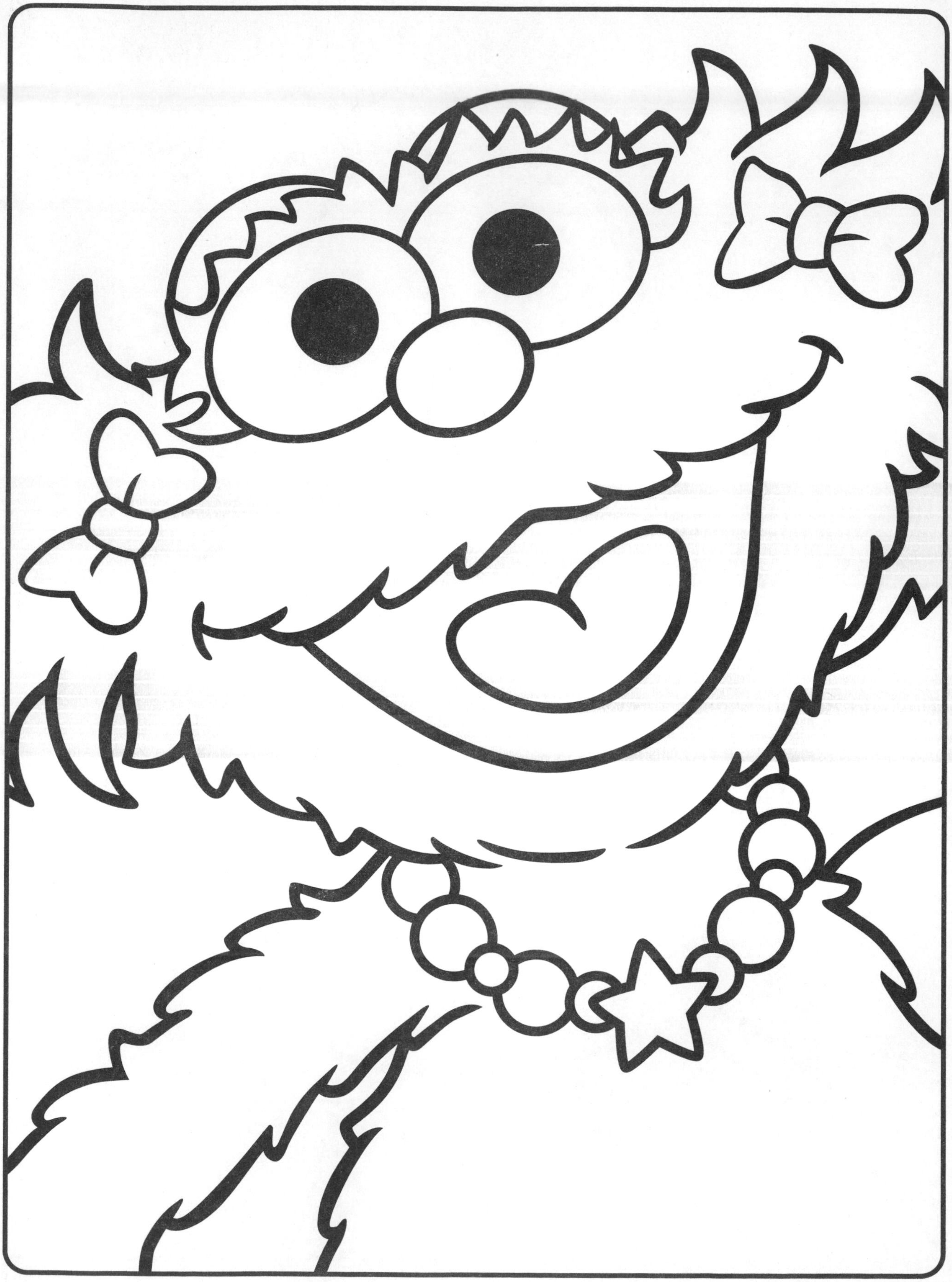

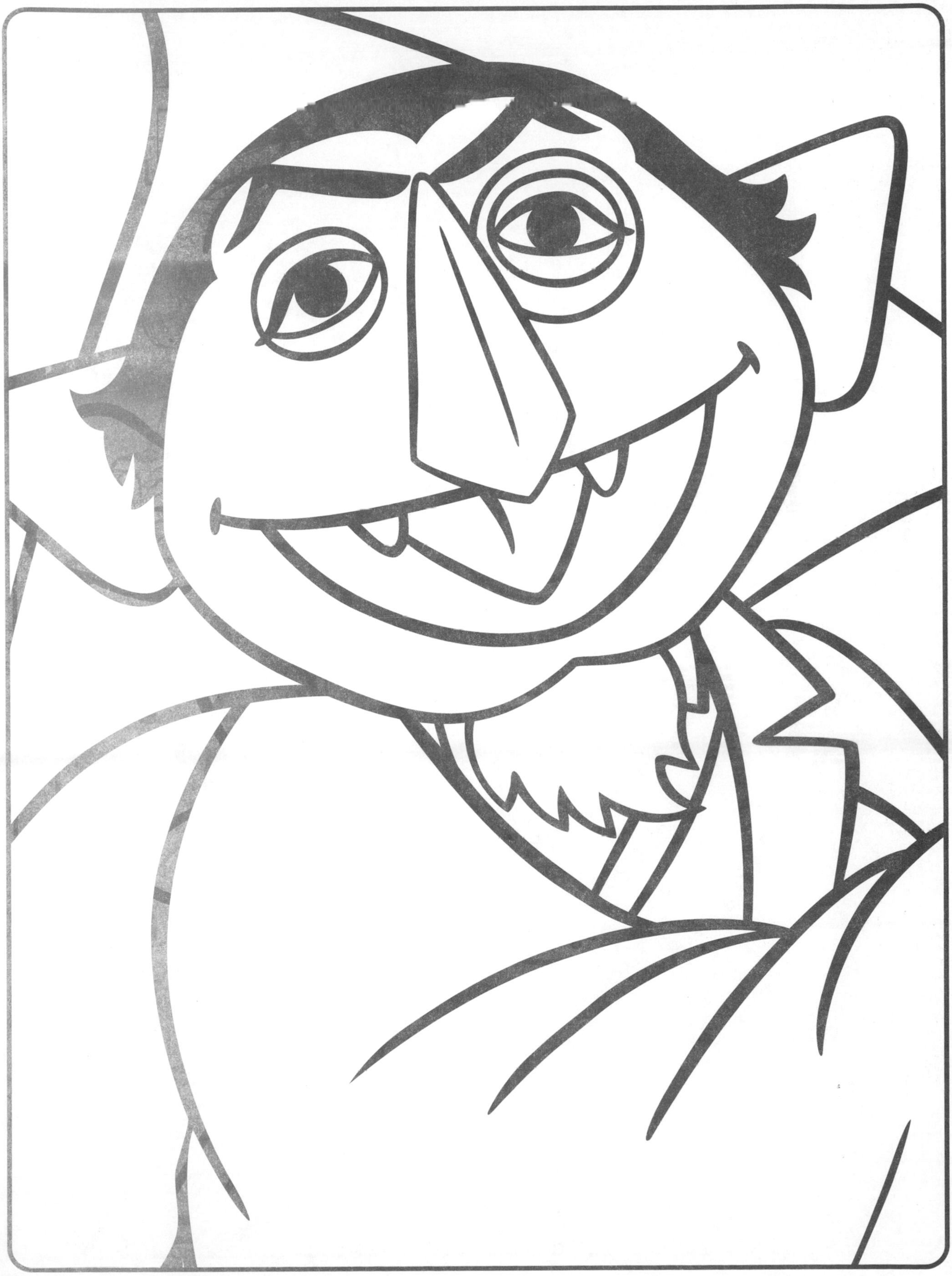

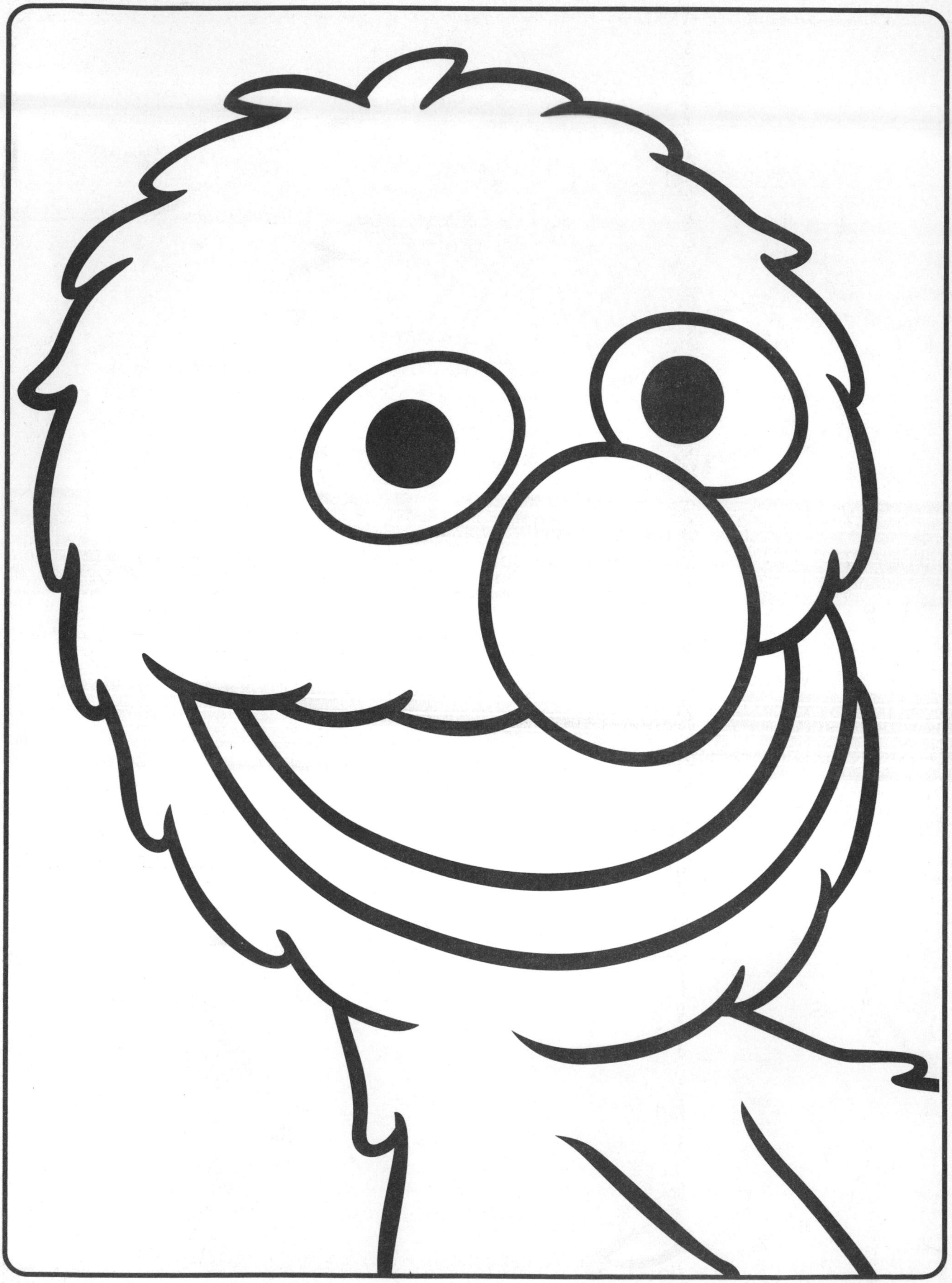

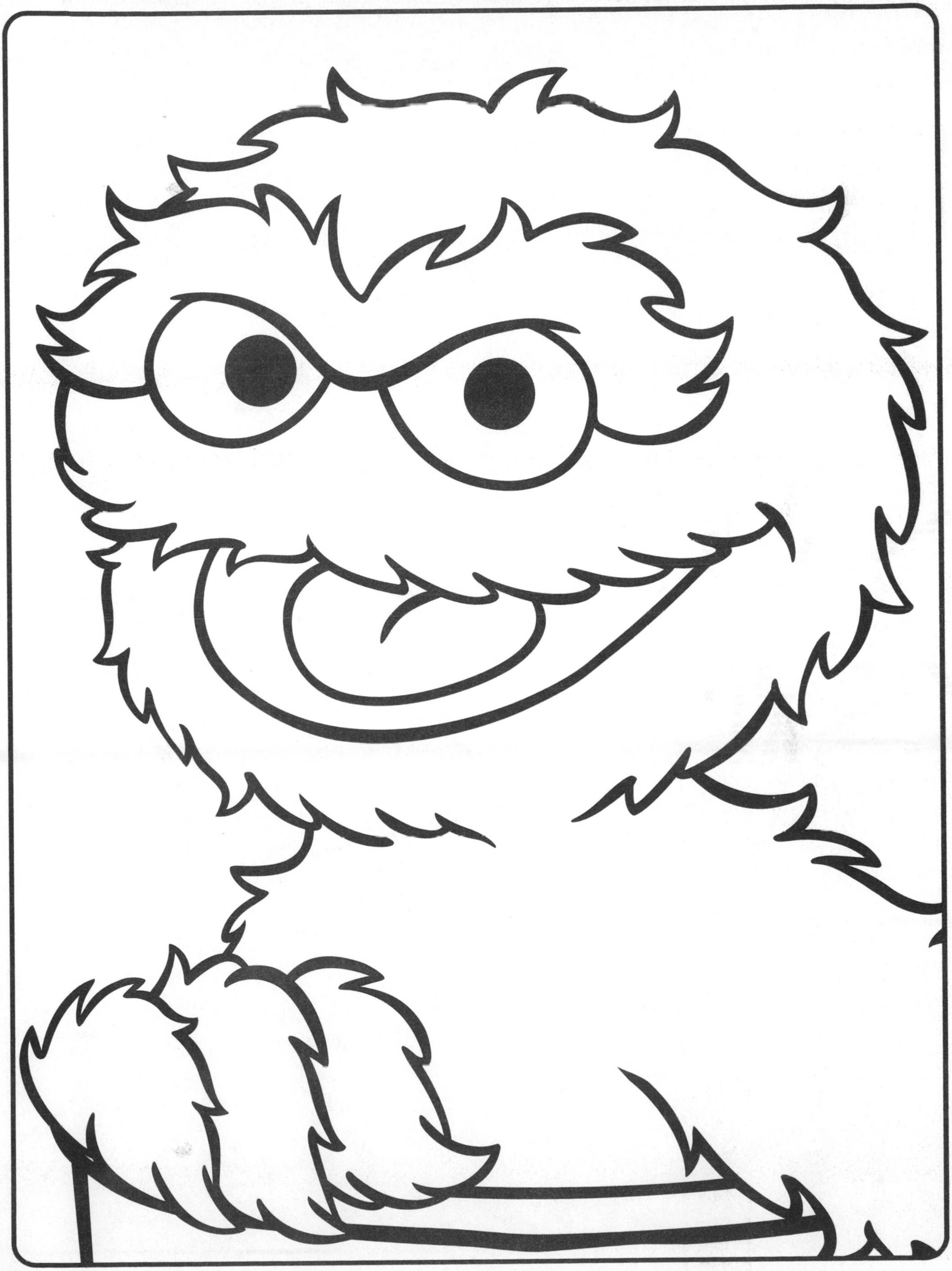

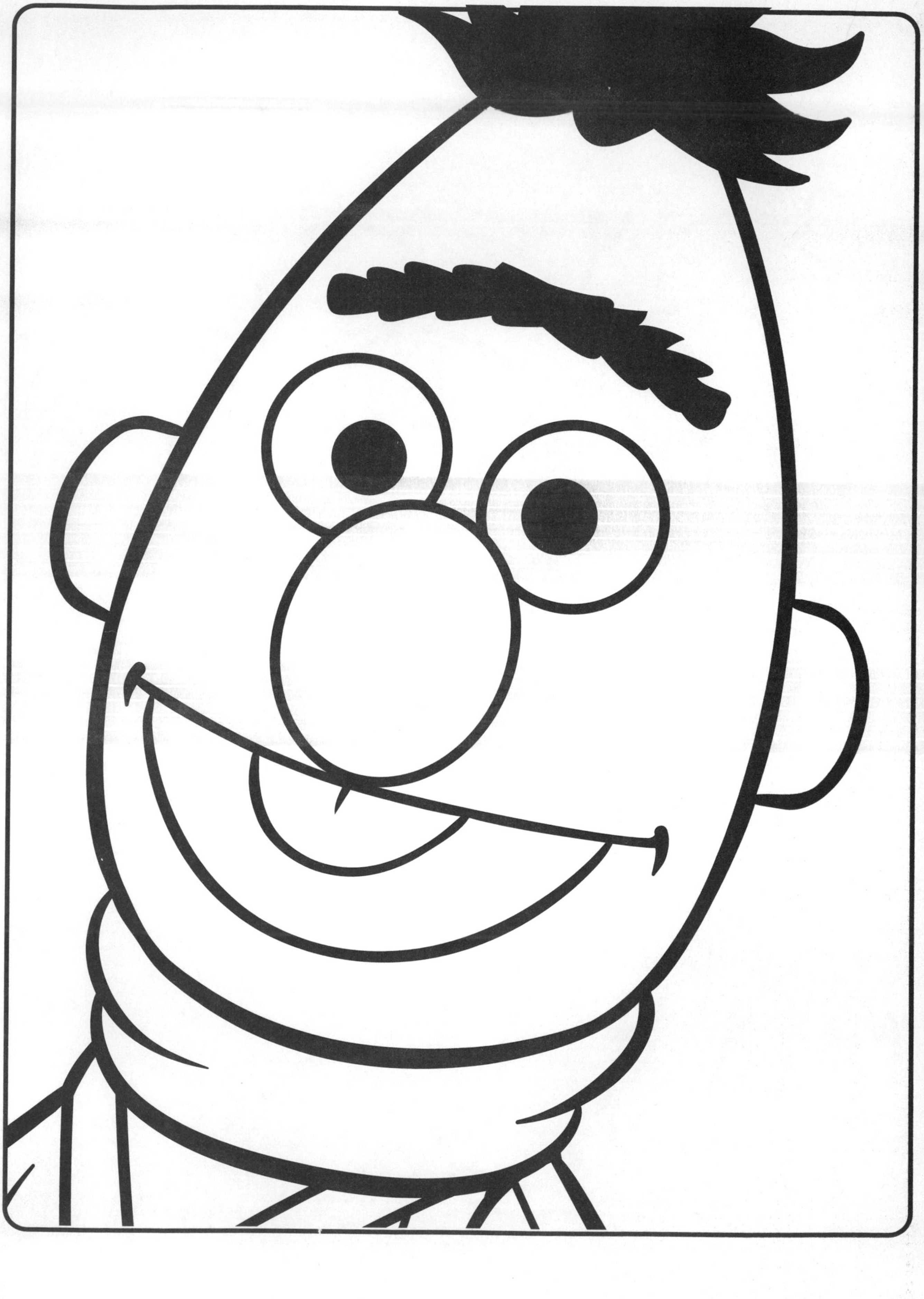

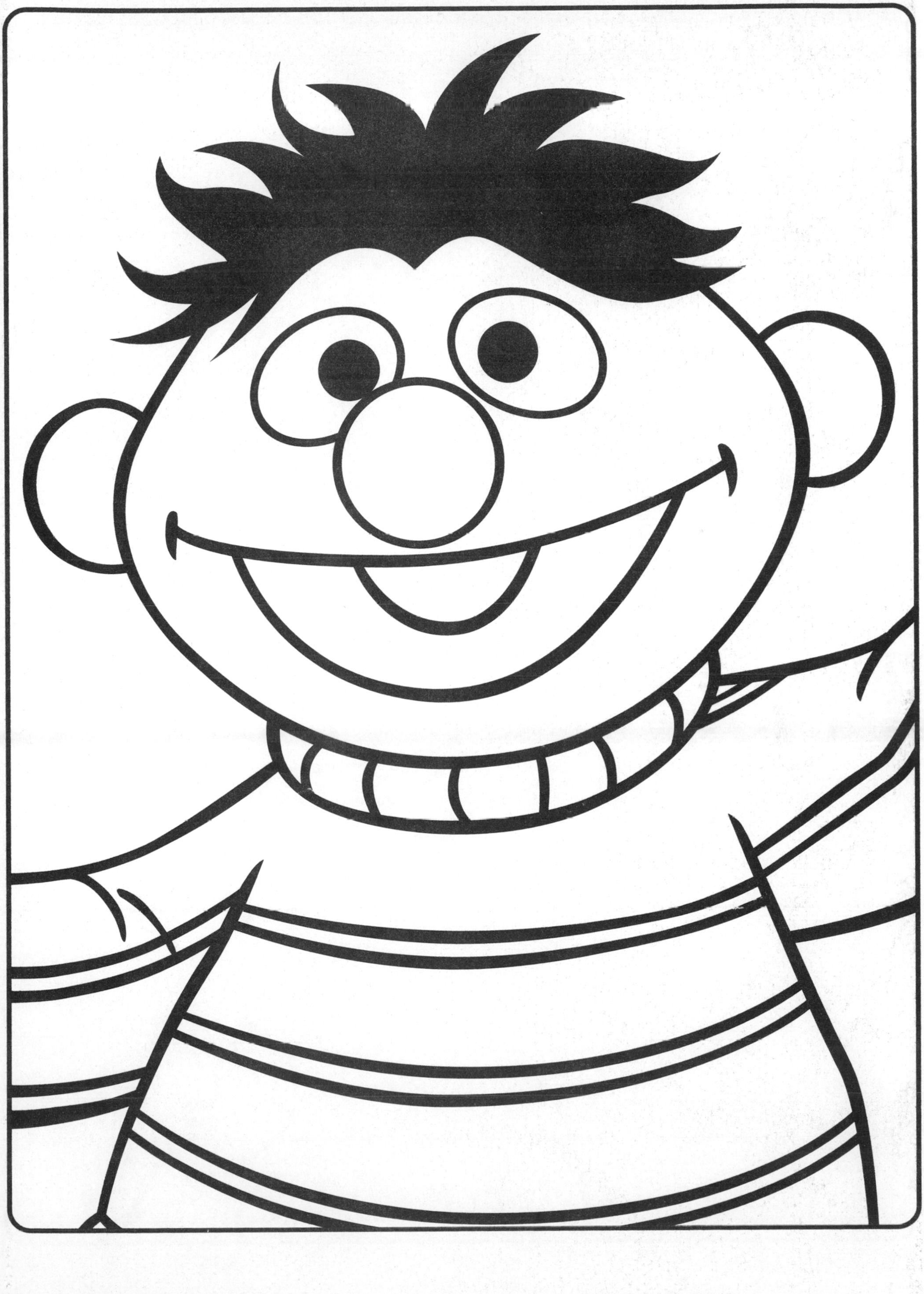

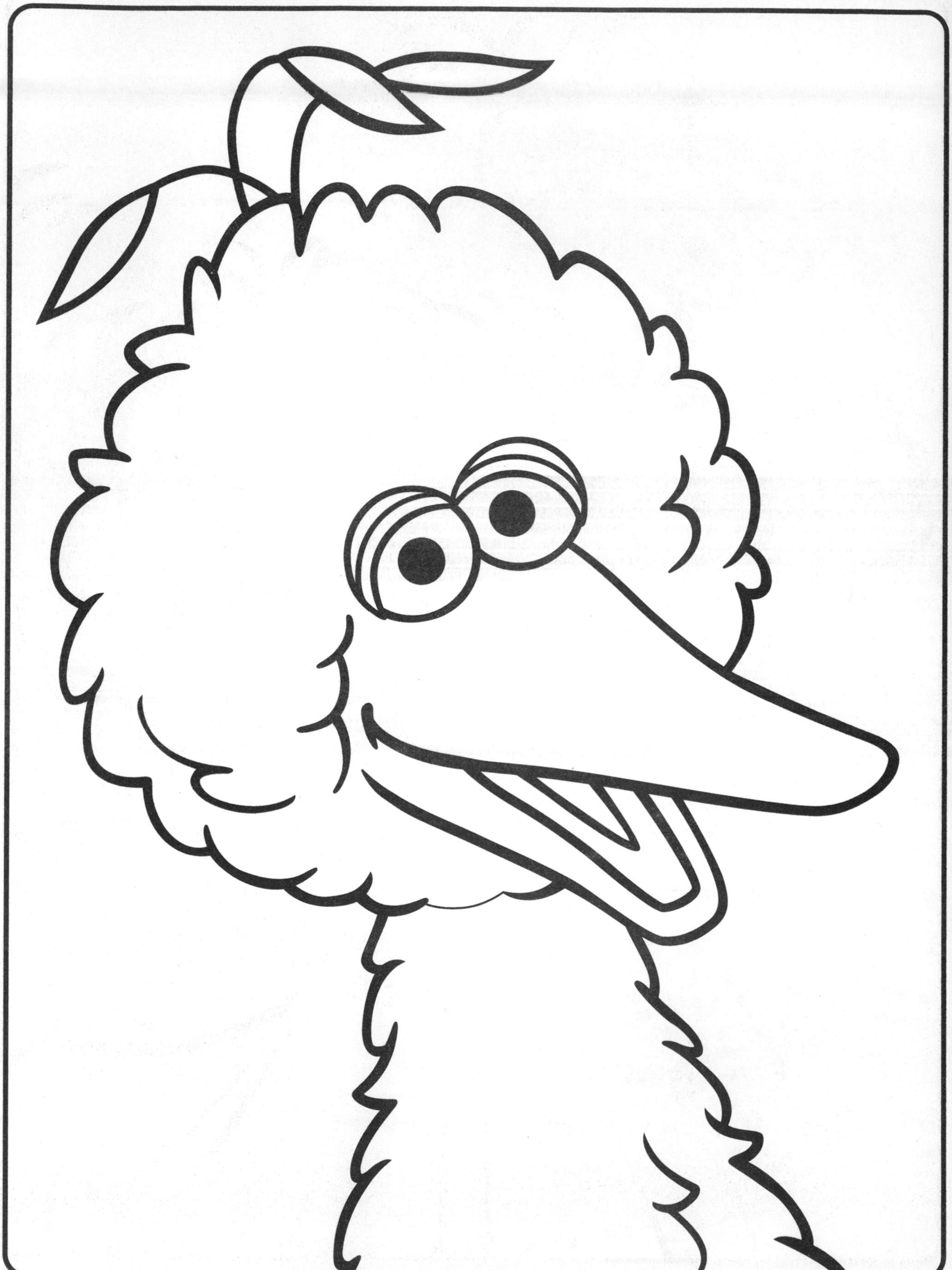

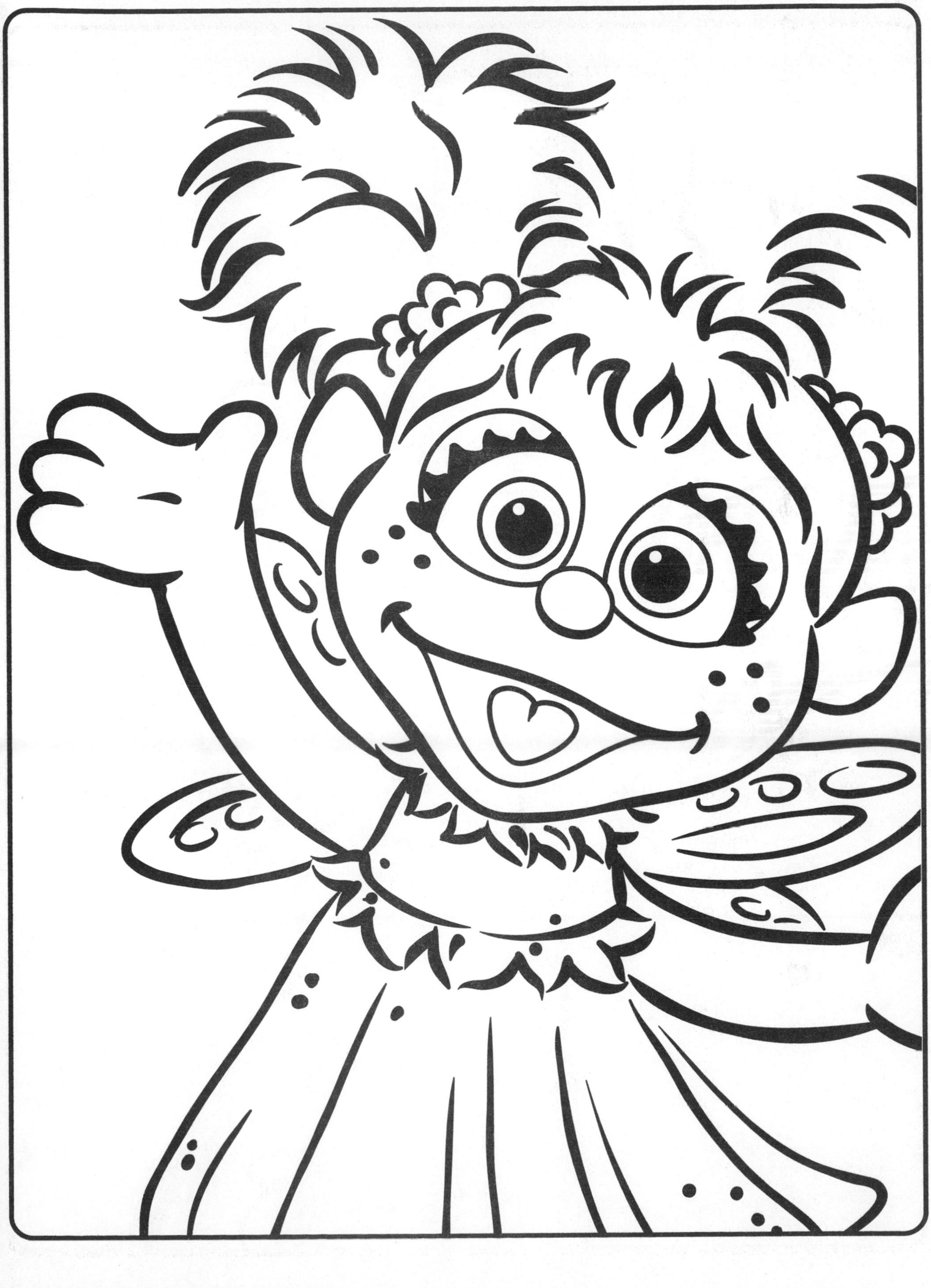

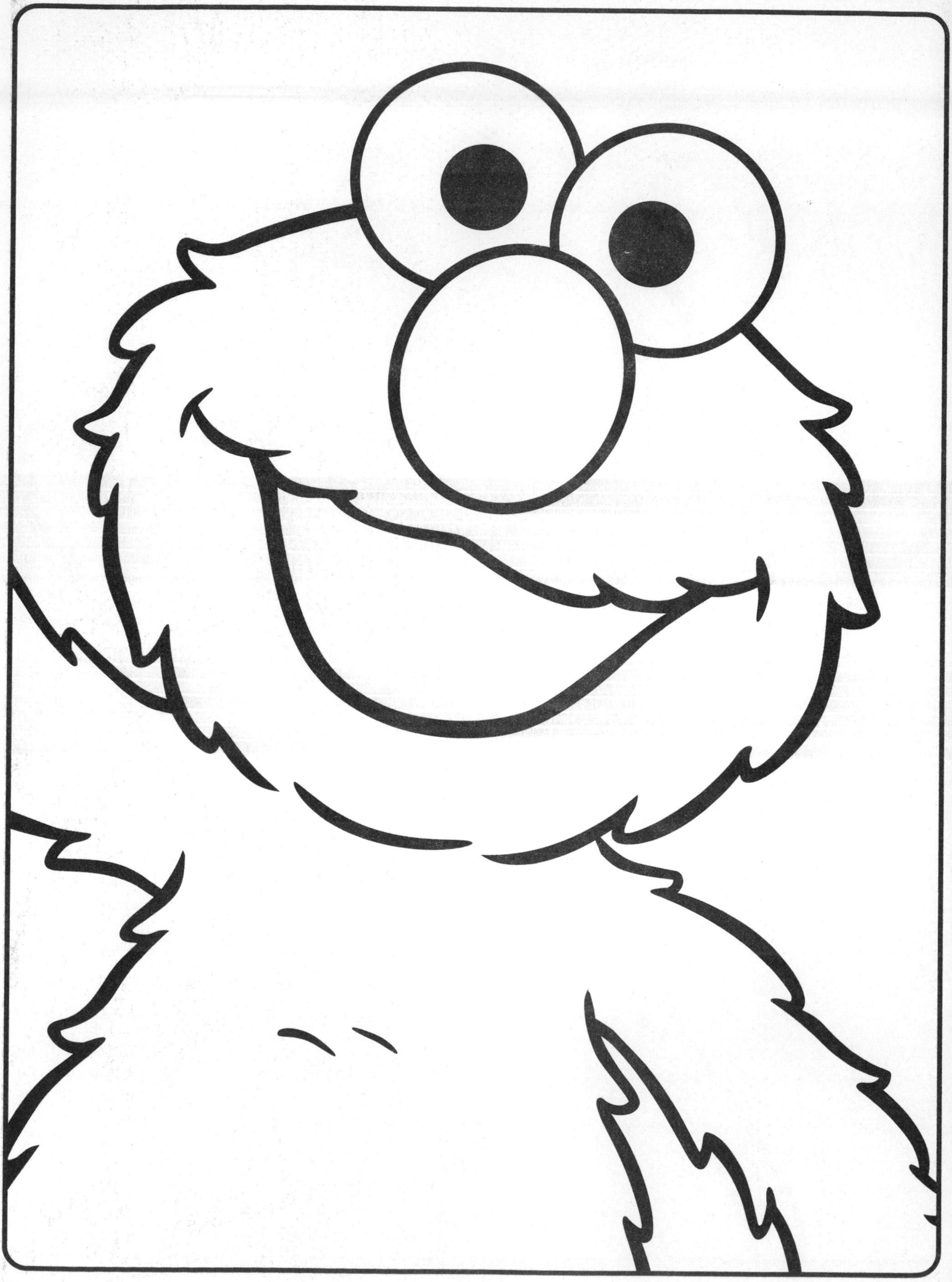

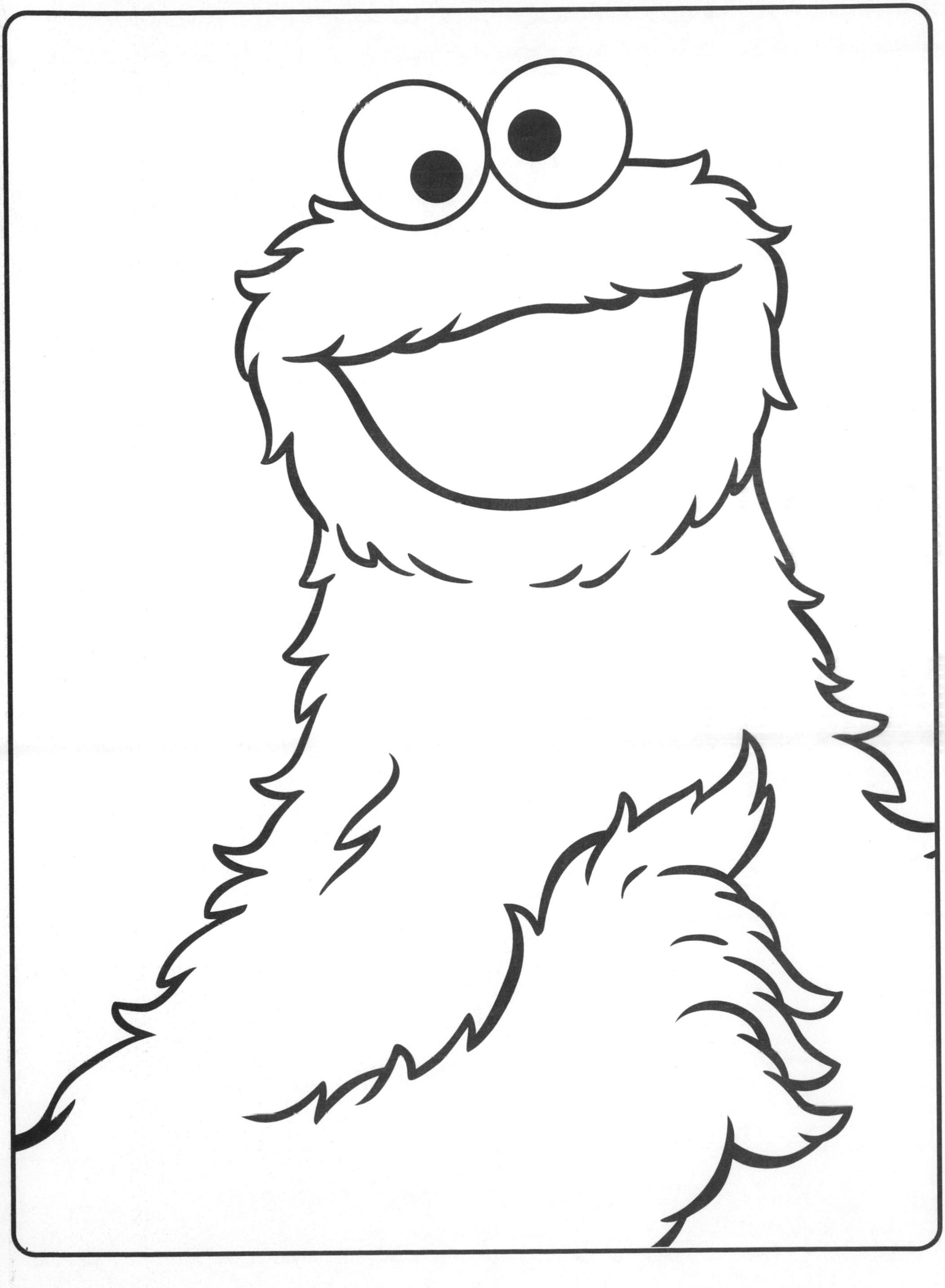

Storytime! Learning Time!

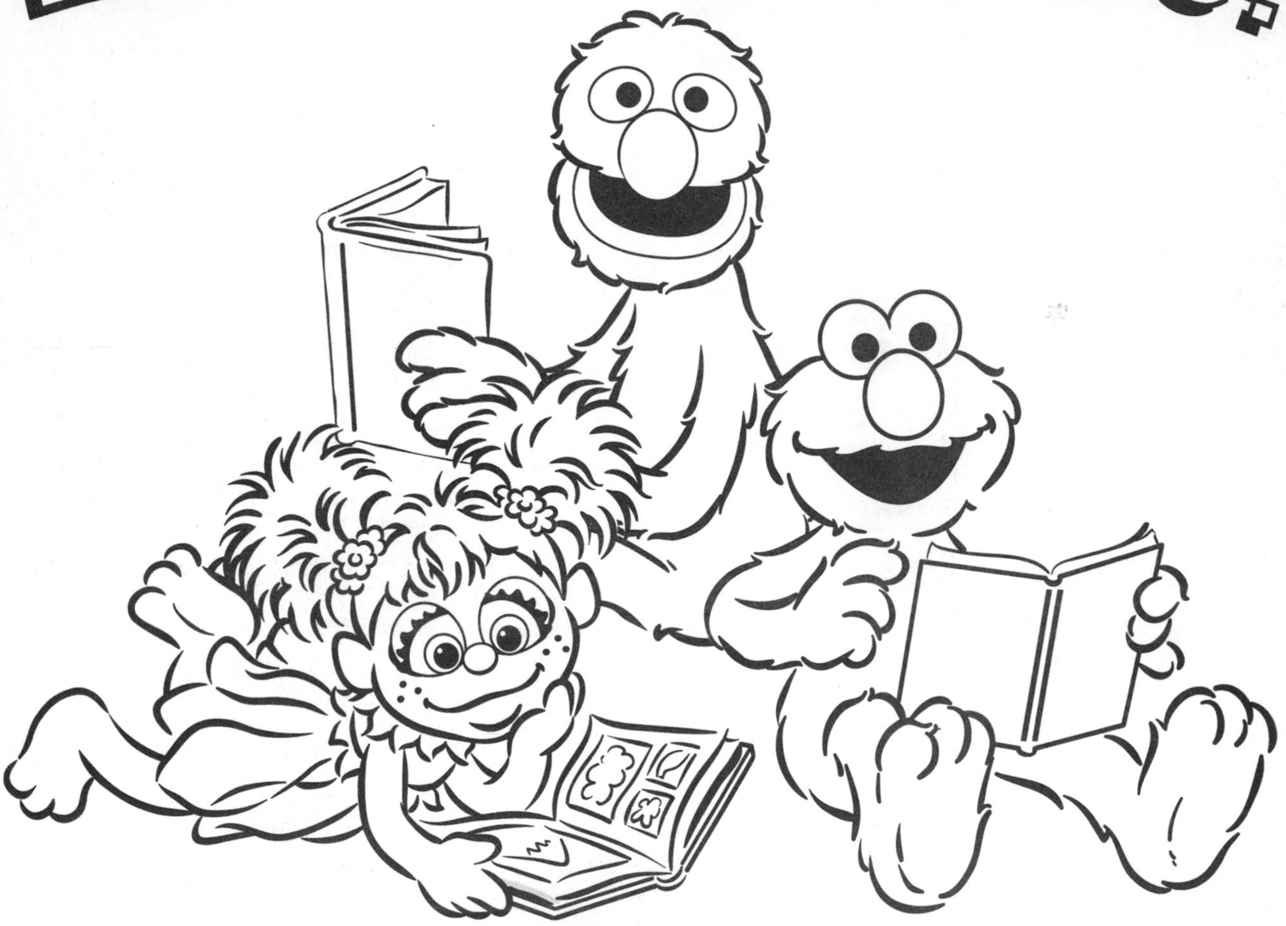

For more learning fun with Elmo and friends, check out the Sesame Street eBookstore at

www.ebooks.sesamestreet.org